T0276276

Baking for Fun

75 Great Cookies, Cakes, Pies & More

HEARST
HOME

Food Network Magazine

Editorial Director Maile Carpenter
Creative Director Deirdre Koribanick
Executive Director Liz Sgroi
Executive Managing Editor Robb Riedel
Photo Director Alice Albert
Special Projects Editor Pamela Mitchell
Deputy Food Editor Teri Tsang Barrett
Book Designer Libby Lang

EDITORIAL
Market Director Kate Doherty
Deputy Features Editor Juliana LaBianca
Online Editorial Coordinator Sabrina Choudhary

ART AND PHOTOGRAPHY
Design Director Ridge Carpenter
Art Director Scott Dvorin
Deputy Art Director Lou DiLorenzo
Senior Designers Hope Johnson, Alexis Walter
Associate Photo Editor Kristen Hazzard
Photo Assistant Yasmeen Yuna Bae
Digital Imaging Specialist Matthew Montesano

COPY
Copy & Research Chief Chris Jagger
Senior Copy Editor David Cobb Craig
Editorial Business Manager Mariah Schlossmann

FOOD NETWORK KITCHEN
Test Kitchen Director Stephen Jackson
Recipe Developers Young Sun Huh, Khalil Hymore, Amy Stevenson

HEARST BOOKS
Vice President & Publisher Jacqueline Deval
Deputy Director Nicole Fisher
Deputy Managing Editor Maria Ramroop
Marketing & Sales Coordinator Nicole Plonski

HEARST MAGAZINE MEDIA, INC.
President Debi Chirichella
Global Chief Revenue Officer Lisa Ryan Howard
Editorial Director Lucy Kaylin
Chief Financial & Strategy Officer; Treasurer Regina Buckley
Consumer Growth Officer Lindsay Horrigan
President, Hearst Magazines International Jonathan Wright
Secretary Catherine A. Bostron
Publishing Consultants Gilbert C. Maurer, Mark F. Miller

HEARST
President & Chief Executive Officer Steven R. Swartz
Chairman William R. Hearst III
Executive Vice Chairman Frank A. Bennack, Jr.

Book design by Libby Lang.

Library of Congress Cataloging-in-Publication Data is available.

10 9 8 7 6 5 4 3 2 1

Published by Hearst Home, an imprint of
Hearst Books/Hearst Communications, Inc.
300 West 57th Street
New York, NY 10019

Food Network Magazine and the Food Network Magazine logo are registered trademarks of Television Food Network, G.P.

Hearst Home, the Hearst Home logo, and Hearst Books are registered trademarks of Hearst Communications, Inc.

For information about custom editions, special sales, premium and corporate purchases: hearst.com/magazines/hearst-books

Printed in China.

ISBN 978-1-958395-22-6

Check out our other books!

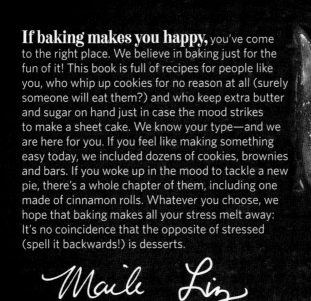

If baking makes you happy, you've come to the right place. We believe in baking just for the fun of it! This book is full of recipes for people like you, who whip up cookies for no reason at all (surely someone will eat them?) and who keep extra butter and sugar on hand just in case the mood strikes to make a sheet cake. We know your type—and we are here for you. If you feel like making something easy today, we included dozens of cookies, brownies and bars. If you woke up in the mood to tackle a new pie, there's a whole chapter of them, including one made of cinnamon rolls. Whatever you choose, we hope that baking makes all your stress melt away: It's no coincidence that the opposite of stressed (spell it backwards!) is desserts.

Maile

Maile Carpenter
Editorial Director

Liz

Liz Sgroi
Executive Director

Contents

Cookies

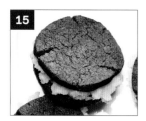
15
Red Velvet
Sandwich Cookies

17
Peanut Butter Mochi
Cookies

19
Blood Orange–Vanilla
Cookies

21
Coconut Cheesecake
Thumbprints

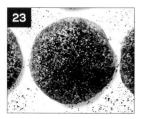
23
Chocolate-Hazelnut
Snowball Cookies

25
Toasted Marshmallow
Sandwich Cookies

27
Pistachio-Chocolate
Meringues

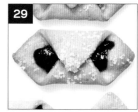
29
Cream Cheese Cookies
with Jam

31
Italian Lemon
Sandwich Cookies

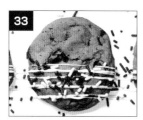
33
Coffee-Toffee
Chocolate Chip Cookies

35
Pumpkin Spice Latte
Whoopie Pies

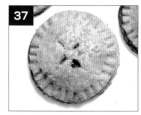
37
Plum Pie Cookies

39
Strawberry Macarons

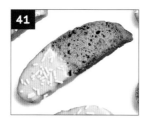
41
Ginger-Maple Biscotti

43
Chai Meringue Drops

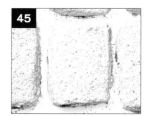
45
Cinnamon-Almond
Melt-Aways

Brownies & Bars

Classic Lemon Bars

Frosted Coffee Brownies

Beer-Spiked Brownies with Pecan Icing

Salted Pretzel Marshmallow Bars

Piña Colada Cheesecake Bars

Snickerdoodle Ice Cream Sandwiches

Key Lime Pie Macaroon Bars

Air-Fryer Pecan Brownies

Strawberry-Walnut Blondies

Maple-Walnut Blondies

Mochi Brownies

Dark Chocolate Pecan Bars

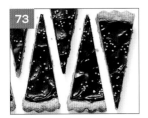
Chocolate-Covered Shortbread

Red Velvet Cheesecake Brownies

Cupcakes

Chocolate Egg Cream
Cupcakes

Chocolate-Bacon
Cupcakes with
Dulce de Leche Frosting

Lemon Meringue
Cupcakes

Orange Cream Cupcakes

Chocolate Ganache
Cupcakes

Banana Pudding Cupcakes

Negroni Cupcakes

Champagne-Vanilla
Cupcakes

Carrot-Walnut Cupcakes

Raspberry-Rose Cupcakes

Peaches-and-Cream
Cupcakes

Piña Colada Cupcakes

Pumpkin Cupcakes with
Toasted Marshmallow
Frosting

Jelly Doughnut Cupcakes

Caramel Corn Cupcakes

Cakes

111

Red Velvet–Cream Cheese Bundt Cake

113

Nectarine Upside-Down Cake with Salted Caramel

115

Rosemary Angel Food Cake with Pineapple Compote

117

Lemon-Vanilla Cake Roll

119

Double Chocolate Cake

121

Coconut Layer Cake

123

Pistachio-Ricotta Cheesecake

125

Chocolate-Cherry Sheet Cake

127

Tiramisu Layer Cake

129

Gluten-Free Toffee Cake

131

Towering Flourless Chocolate Cake

133

Glazed Raspberry Crumb Cake

135

Triple Chocolate Cheesecake

137

Carrot Cake with Orange Marmalade

139

Spicy Texas Sheet Cake

Pies & Tarts

143
Banana Pudding Tart

145
Mile-High S'mores Pie

147
PB&J Tart

149
Puff Pastry Berry Cheesecake Tart

151
Grape Galette with Almond Cream

153
Cinnamon Bun Apple Pie

155
Chocolate-Toffee Pecan Tart

157
Poppy Seed Tart

159
Peach Custard Pie

161
Sugar Cream Pie

163
Spiced Cherry-Berry Slab Pie

165
Pear-Walnut Chocolate Tart

167
Classic Lemon Tart

169
Peach Hand Pies

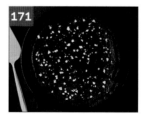
171
Dark Chocolate–Caramel Tart

Cookies

If you leave cookies on a hot baking sheet, they'll continue cooking. Let them cool for just a few minutes, then transfer to a cooling rack.

Red Velvet Sandwich Cookies

ACTIVE: 35 min I TOTAL: 3 hr (plus cooling) I MAKES: about 16

FOR THE COOKIES

1 cup all-purpose flour

1 tablespoon unsweetened dutch-process cocoa powder

¼ teaspoon baking soda

Pinch of salt

6 tablespoons unsalted butter, at room temperature

¾ cup confectioners' sugar

½ teaspoon pure vanilla extract

1 teaspoon red food coloring

FOR THE FILLING

¾ cup sweetened shredded coconut

4 ounces cream cheese, at room temperature

⅓ cup confectioners' sugar

Pinch of salt

½ teaspoon pure vanilla extract

1 Make the cookies: Whisk together the flour, cocoa powder, baking soda and salt in a medium bowl. Beat the butter, confectioners' sugar and vanilla in a large bowl with a mixer on medium speed until smooth, about 1 minute. Reduce the mixer speed to low and beat in the flour mixture in 2 additions. Add the food coloring and beat until combined. Transfer the dough to a clean surface and knead a few times. Roll into a 10-inch-long, 1-inch-diameter log; wrap in plastic wrap and freeze until firm, about 2 hours.

2 Meanwhile, make the filling: Pulse the coconut, cream cheese, confectioners' sugar, salt and vanilla in a food processor until combined. Refrigerate until ready to use.

3 Position racks in the upper and lower thirds of the oven; preheat to 350°. Line 2 baking sheets with parchment paper. Remove the dough from the freezer and unwrap. Slice the dough into ¼-inch-thick rounds and arrange about 1 inch apart on the baking sheets. Bake, switching the pans halfway through, until the cookies are firm around the edges, 8 to 10 minutes. Let cool 2 minutes on the baking sheets, then transfer to a rack to cool completely.

4 Spread about 1 teaspoon of the filling on the flat side of half of the cookies. Sandwich with the remaining cookies.

This recipe calls for glutinous rice flour. You can also use it to make the mochi brownies on page 69.

Peanut Butter Mochi Cookies

ACTIVE: 1 hr I TOTAL: 1½ hr (plus cooling) I MAKES: 24

FOR THE COOKIES

1½ cups all-purpose flour

1 teaspoon baking soda

1 teaspoon kosher salt

1 stick unsalted butter, at room temperature

½ cup granulated sugar, plus more for rolling

½ cup packed light brown sugar

½ cup creamy peanut butter (not natural)

1 large egg

1½ teaspoons pure vanilla extract

FOR THE FILLING

¾ cup mochiko (glutinous rice flour or sweet rice flour)

⅓ cup confectioners' sugar

¼ teaspoon kosher salt

¾ cup whole milk, warmed

1 tablespoon unsalted butter, melted

½ teaspoon pure vanilla extract

Cooking spray

FOR THE GLAZE

¾ cup creamy peanut butter (not natural)

¼ cup confectioners' sugar

1 Make the cookies: Position racks in the upper and lower thirds of the oven; preheat to 350°. Line 2 baking sheets with parchment paper. Whisk the all-purpose flour, baking soda and salt in a medium bowl.

2 Beat the butter, granulated sugar and brown sugar in a large bowl with a mixer on medium speed until pale and fluffy, about 4 minutes. Beat in the peanut butter until well combined, about 2 more minutes. Beat in the egg and vanilla. Reduce the mixer speed to low and beat in the flour mixture until just combined.

3 Scoop the dough into 24 balls (a 1-ounce cookie scoop works well for this). Roll the balls with your hands until smooth, then roll in granulated sugar. Arrange about 2 inches apart on the baking sheets. Refrigerate while preparing the filling.

4 Make the filling: Whisk the mochiko, confectioners' sugar and salt in a medium microwave-safe bowl. Whisk in the warm milk and melted butter until smooth; whisk in the vanilla. Microwave in 30-second intervals, stirring in between, until the mixture is smooth but sticky and holds together in a ball, 1 to 2 minutes. Let cool slightly. Lightly coat a teaspoon-size measuring spoon with cooking spray and scoop 24 rounded heaping balls of filling, placing them on a clean work surface. Lightly coat your hands with cooking spray and roll the balls until smooth. Flatten each ball slightly to make a disk.

5 Bake the chilled cookies, switching the pans halfway through, until lightly golden and puffed, 8 to 12 minutes. Remove from the oven and quickly press a measuring spoon into the center of each to create an indentation. Place a filling disk into each indentation. Return to the oven and bake until the filling softens, 3 to 6 more minutes. Let the cookies cool 5 minutes on the baking sheets, then transfer to a rack to cool completely.

6 Make the glaze: Put the peanut butter in a medium microwave-safe bowl and microwave in 10-second intervals, stirring, until thin enough to drizzle, 30 seconds. Whisk in the confectioners' sugar. Drizzle on the cookies and let set.

Blood Orange-Vanilla Cookies

ACTIVE: 40 min | TOTAL: 3 hr (plus cooling) | MAKES: about 30

FOR THE COOKIES

2 sticks unsalted butter, at room temperature

2½ cups all-purpose flour

1 cup confectioners' sugar

½ teaspoon salt

1 tablespoon blood orange zest (or Cara Cara or navel orange zest)

1 tablespoon vanilla bean paste

2 teaspoons orange extract

FOR THE ROYAL ICING

1 pound confectioners' sugar

2 tablespoons meringue powder

4 to 6 tablespoons blood orange juice (or Cara Cara or navel orange juice)

2 teaspoons pure vanilla extract

2 teaspoons orange extract

Orange and red gel food coloring

> Royal icing hardens as it dries thanks to the meringue powder. Let the icing set for at least an hour.

1 Make the cookies: Beat the butter in a large bowl with a mixer on medium-high speed until light and fluffy, about 3 minutes. In a small bowl, whisk together the flour, confectioners' sugar and salt. Reduce the mixer speed to low, then beat the flour mixture into the butter mixture until just combined. Stir in the orange zest, vanilla bean paste and orange extract. Divide the dough into 2 balls, then form into disks and wrap in plastic wrap; refrigerate until firm, at least 1 hour.

2 Position racks in the upper and lower thirds of the oven; preheat to 325°. Line 2 baking sheets with parchment paper. On a lightly floured surface, roll out 1 disk of dough until just shy of ¼ inch thick; if the dough cracks, let it warm up a few minutes. Cut out rounds with a 2½- to 3-inch cutter, then arrange about 1 inch apart on one of the baking sheets. Gather the scraps and reroll to cut out more cookies; refrigerate 10 minutes before baking.

3 Bake, switching the pans halfway through, until the cookies are lightly golden, 12 to 14 minutes. Let cool 5 minutes on the baking sheets, then transfer to a rack to cool completely. Meanwhile, repeat with the remaining disk of dough.

4 Make the royal icing: Mix together the confectioners' sugar, meringue powder, 4 tablespoons blood orange juice and both extracts until the icing is spreadable and not runny; if it's too thick, whisk in more juice, 1 tablespoon at a time. Transfer 1 cup of the icing to a small bowl and mix with orange and red food coloring to make a blood orange color. Drizzle some of the colored icing over the plain icing; swirl slightly with a toothpick or skewer. Dip the tops of the cookies into the icing, gently twisting to create a marbled effect; allow the excess to drip off. Transfer the cookies to a rack set on a baking sheet. Let the icing set at least 1 hour.

Coconut Cheesecake Thumbprints

ACTIVE: 35 min **I** TOTAL: 1 hr 45 min (plus cooling) **I** MAKES: 28 to 30

FOR THE COOKIES

- 1¾ cups all-purpose flour
- ½ teaspoon baking powder
- ½ teaspoon salt
- 1 stick unsalted butter, at room temperature
- 4 ounces cream cheese, at room temperature
- 1 cup granulated sugar
- 1 teaspoon finely grated lime zest
- 1 large egg yolk
- 1 teaspoon pure vanilla extract
- 1 teaspoon coconut extract
- ¾ cup sweetened shredded coconut

FOR THE FILLING

- 2 ounces cream cheese, at room temperature
- 2 tablespoons sour cream
- ½ cup confectioners' sugar
- ½ teaspoon pure vanilla extract
- ¼ teaspoon coconut extract

1 Make the cookies: Whisk together the flour, baking powder and salt in a medium bowl. Beat the butter, cream cheese, granulated sugar and lime zest in a large bowl with a mixer on medium-high speed until fluffy and smooth, 2 to 3 minutes. Add the egg yolk and both extracts and mix until combined. Reduce the speed to low. Beat in the flour mixture in 2 batches until just combined. Refrigerate until firm, about 1 hour.

2 Meanwhile, make the filling: Combine the cream cheese, sour cream, confectioners' sugar and both extracts in a medium bowl. Whisk together until smooth (the mixture will be stiff but will loosen as you whisk).

3 Position racks in the upper and lower thirds of the oven; preheat to 350°. Line 2 baking sheets with parchment paper. Place the shredded coconut in a small bowl, breaking up any large clumps. Scoop heaping tablespoons of dough about 1½ inches apart onto the baking sheets. Roll each into a ball and dip the top half in the coconut to generously coat. Make a deep indentation in the center of each ball using a ½-teaspoon measuring spoon. Fill with the cream cheese filling.

4 Bake, rotating and switching the pans halfway through, until the cookies are golden on the bottom and some coconut has browned on top, 14 to 16 minutes. Let the cookies cool 2 minutes on the pans, then transfer to a rack to cool completely.

A ½-teaspoon measuring spoon is perfect for making an indentation in thumbprint cookies. You can also use the handle of a wooden spoon.

Chocolate-Hazelnut Snowball Cookies

ACTIVE: 45 min **I** TOTAL: 2 hr (plus cooling) **I** MAKES: about 24

½ cup blanched hazelnuts

1¾ cups all-purpose flour

⅓ cup unsweetened cocoa powder, plus more for dusting

¼ teaspoon salt

2 sticks unsalted butter, at room temperature

1½ cups confectioners' sugar

1 teaspoon pure vanilla extract

4 ounces bittersweet chocolate, finely chopped

1 Position racks in the upper and lower thirds of the oven; preheat to 350°. Spread the hazelnuts on a baking sheet and bake on the lower rack until lightly toasted, about 10 minutes. Let cool completely, about 20 minutes.

2 Pulse the hazelnuts in a food processor until finely ground. Add the flour, cocoa powder and salt and pulse to combine.

3 Beat the butter in a large bowl with a mixer on medium-high speed until light and fluffy, about 3 minutes. Add ½ cup confectioners' sugar and the vanilla; beat on low speed until combined, then increase the speed to medium-high and beat until well combined. Reduce the speed to low again, add the flour mixture and beat until combined. Beat in the chopped chocolate. Cover the dough and refrigerate until slightly firm, about 30 minutes.

4 Scoop heaping tablespoons of dough and roll into balls. Arrange 2 inches apart on 2 unlined baking sheets. Bake, switching the pans halfway through, until the cookies have a matte finish and look slightly darker around the edges, 18 to 24 minutes. Let the cookies cool on the pans 5 minutes, then transfer to a rack to cool completely.

5 Put the remaining 1 cup confectioners' sugar in a bowl. Gently roll the cookies in the sugar to coat completely, rerolling as needed. Dust the cookies with cocoa powder.

When grinding nuts in a food processor, be careful not to go too far. If you overprocess, you'll end up with nut butter!

Toasted Marshmallow Sandwich Cookies

ACTIVE: 50 min I TOTAL: 3 hr (plus cooling) I MAKES: 12

Cooking spray

25 marshmallows

1¾ cups all-purpose flour

1 teaspoon baking powder

½ teaspoon salt

1 stick unsalted butter, at room temperature

½ cup granulated sugar

1 large egg

1 teaspoon pure vanilla extract

½ cup white sanding sugar

½ cup marshmallow cream

> The marshmallow cream in these cookies is very sticky. Coat your spoon with cooking spray before you scoop it so it slides off easily.

1 Preheat the broiler. Line a baking sheet with foil and lightly coat with cooking spray. Spread the marshmallows on the baking sheet and broil, flipping halfway through, until puffed and toasted (but not charred), 1½ to 2 minutes. Let cool.

2 Meanwhile, whisk the flour, baking powder and salt in a bowl. Beat the butter and granulated sugar in a large bowl with a mixer on medium-high speed until light and fluffy, 3 to 5 minutes. Add the egg and vanilla and beat until smooth, about 1 minute, scraping down the bowl as needed. Add the cooled toasted marshmallows and stir with a rubber spatula, smashing in the marshmallows until incorporated (a few marshmallow lumps are fine). Add the flour mixture and stir until just combined. Cover the dough and refrigerate until no longer sticky, 2 to 4 hours.

3 Position racks in the upper and lower thirds of the oven; preheat to 350°. Line 2 baking sheets with parchment paper. Spread the sanding sugar in a shallow bowl. Scoop the chilled dough into 24 balls, about 1½ tablespoons each. Roll in the sugar and arrange about 2 inches apart on the baking sheets. Bake, rotating and switching the pans halfway through, until the cookies are set and golden around the edges, 10 to 15 minutes. Let cool 3 to 5 minutes on the pans, then transfer to a rack to cool completely.

4 Turn over half the cookies so the flat side is up. Top each with about 2 teaspoons marshmallow cream. Let stand 5 minutes so the marshmallow starts to spread, then top with a second cookie, flat-side down. Gently press and let stand about 10 minutes; the marshmallow cream will spread to the edge.

Pistachio-Chocolate Meringues

ACTIVE: 45 min **I** TOTAL: 1½ hr (plus cooling) **I** MAKES: about 30

- ¾ cup plus 2 tablespoons raw pistachios
- ¾ cup sugar
- 3 large egg whites, at room temperature
- ¼ teaspoon cream of tartar
- ¼ teaspoon salt
- 1 teaspoon pure vanilla extract
- 2 ounces bittersweet chocolate, finely chopped

Egg whites whip up better when they're at room temperature. If your eggs are cold, put them in a bowl, cover with warm water and let them sit 5 minutes before you crack them.

1 Position racks in the upper and lower thirds of the oven; preheat to 350˚. Spread ¾ cup pistachios on a baking sheet and bake on the lower rack until toasted, about 8 minutes. Let cool completely, then pulse in a food processor until finely chopped.

2 Line 2 baking sheets with parchment paper. Spread the sugar on one of the pans and bake on the lower rack until very hot but not melting, about 10 minutes. Reduce the oven temperature to 225˚.

3 Meanwhile, combine the egg whites, cream of tartar and salt in the bowl of a stand mixer fitted with the whisk attachment. About 30 seconds before the sugar comes out of the oven, beat the egg whites on medium speed until soft peaks form. Gradually beat in the hot sugar, about 1 tablespoon at a time, using the parchment paper as a funnel. Increase the mixer speed to high and beat, scraping down the bowl as needed, until stiff peaks form, 3 to 4 minutes. Add the vanilla and beat until the meringue is fluffy, about 30 seconds.

4 Reline the baking sheet used for the sugar with parchment paper. Gently fold the chopped pistachios and chocolate into the meringue with a rubber spatula until just combined. Transfer to a piping bag fitted with a ½-inch round tip. Pipe the meringue into 1¾-inch-wide mounds (about 1½ inches tall) about 1 inch apart onto the baking sheets. Very finely chop the remaining 2 tablespoons pistachios, then sprinkle on the meringues.

5 Bake, switching the pans halfway through, until the meringues are firm to the touch and lift easily off the parchment, 40 to 50 minutes. Turn off the oven and let the meringues sit in the oven 10 minutes, then transfer to racks to cool completely.

Cream Cheese Cookies with Jam

ACTIVE: 40 min I TOTAL: 2 hr (plus cooling) I MAKES: about 36

1   8-ounce package
     cream cheese,
     at room temperature
2   sticks unsalted butter,
     at room temperature
3   tablespoons granulated
     sugar
2¾ cups all-purpose flour,
     plus more for dusting
½   teaspoon salt
½   cup apricot preserves
½   cup raspberry preserves
Coarse sugar, for sprinkling

> These cookies
> are a take on
> kolaczki, Polish
> cream cheese cookies.
> The dough is tender
> and flaky, like
> pie dough.

1 Beat the cream cheese, butter and granulated sugar in a large bowl with a mixer on medium-high speed until light and fluffy, about 2 minutes, scraping down the bowl as needed. Reduce the mixer speed to low and beat in the flour and salt until combined. Divide the dough between 2 large pieces of plastic wrap. Flatten into ½-inch-thick disks and wrap. Refrigerate until firm, at least 1 hour or overnight.

2 Preheat the oven to 350°. Line 2 baking sheets with parchment paper. Roll out 1 disk of dough on a lightly floured surface until about ⅛ inch thick, dusting with more flour as needed. Cut out 2½-inch squares using a sharp knife or a 2½-inch square cutter. Lift the cutouts using an offset spatula and arrange 2 inches apart on one of the baking sheets. Gather the scraps and refrigerate.

3 Spoon 1 teaspoon preserves onto the center of each cutout. Fold in 2 opposite corners to overlap in the middle and press down to seal, spreading the preserves slightly. Sprinkle the dough with coarse sugar.

4 Bake, rotating the pan halfway through, until the cookies are puffed and the edges are golden, 20 to 25 minutes. Let the cookies cool 5 minutes on the pan, then transfer to a rack to cool completely. Repeat with the other disk of dough, plus the reserved scraps, to make more cookies.

Italian Lemon Sandwich Cookies

ACTIVE: 50 min I TOTAL: 1 hr 45 min (plus 1 hr setting) I MAKES: about 24

2   cups all-purpose flour

½   teaspoon baking powder

½   teaspoon salt

2   sticks unsalted butter,
     at room temperature

½   cup sugar

1   teaspoon finely grated
     lemon zest

2   large egg yolks

½   teaspoon pure vanilla
     extract

½   teaspoon pure almond
     extract

¼   cup whole milk

¼   cup lemon curd

¾   cup white candy melts
     (about 4 ounces)

3   tablespoons vegetable
     shortening

Nonpareils, for decorating

You don't need a special pan to make these bakery cookies: Just pipe the dough with a star tip.

1 Position racks in the upper and lower thirds of the oven; preheat to 350°. Line 2 baking sheets with parchment paper. Whisk together the flour, baking powder and salt in a medium bowl.

2 Beat the butter, sugar and lemon zest in a large bowl with a mixer on medium-high speed until pale and fluffy, about 2 minutes. Add the egg yolks and vanilla and almond extracts and beat until combined. Reduce the mixer speed to low and gradually beat in the flour mixture until combined, then slowly beat in the milk.

3 Transfer the dough to a piping bag fitted with a ½-inch open star tip. Pipe 1¾-inch logs about 2 inches apart on the prepared pans. (You will have leftover dough.)

4 Bake, switching the pans halfway through, until the cookies are golden around the edges, 18 to 24 minutes. Let the cookies cool 5 minutes on the pans, then transfer to racks to cool completely.

5 Pipe the remaining dough onto one of the used parchment-lined baking sheets; bake only 15 to 20 minutes. Let the cookies cool 5 minutes on the pan, then transfer to a rack to cool completely.

6 Sandwich a thin layer of lemon curd between the cookies (½ teaspoon each). Microwave the candy melts and shortening in a microwave-safe bowl in 30-second intervals, stirring, until smooth. Dip the cookies partway in the candy melts, letting the excess drip off. Return to the racks and top with nonpareils. Let set, about 1 hour.

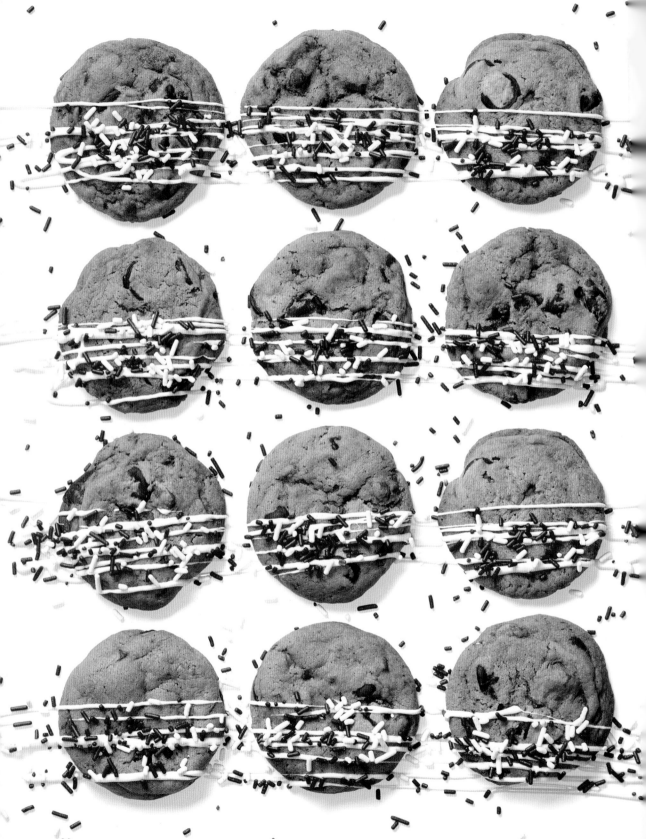

Coffee-Toffee Chocolate Chip Cookies

ACTIVE: 40 min **|** TOTAL: 1 hr 15 min (plus cooling) **|** MAKES: about 24

1¾ cups all-purpose flour

¾ teaspoon baking soda

¾ teaspoon kosher salt

1¼ sticks (10 tablespoons) unsalted butter, at room temperature

1 tablespoon instant espresso powder

1 cup packed light brown sugar

1 large egg

1 teaspoon pure vanilla extract

1 cup dark chocolate chips

3 1.4-ounce chocolate-toffee bars, chopped (about 1 cup)

1 cup white chocolate chips

Sprinkles, for decorating

1 Preheat the oven to 375°. Line 2 baking sheets with parchment paper. Whisk together the flour, baking soda and salt in a medium bowl.

2 Beat the butter, espresso powder and brown sugar in a large bowl with a mixer on medium-high speed until light and fluffy, about 3 minutes. Beat in the egg and vanilla until smooth. Reduce the mixer speed to low, then gradually beat in the flour mixture until just combined. Stir in the dark chocolate chips and toffee bars.

3 Roll the dough into 1½-inch balls and arrange 2 inches apart on the baking sheets. Bake, switching the pans halfway through, until the cookies are puffed and just set around the edges, about 15 minutes. Let the cookies cool 10 minutes on the pans, then transfer to a rack to cool completely.

4 Melt the white chocolate chips in the microwave in 15-second intervals, stirring, until smooth. Drizzle over one side of each cookie and decorate with sprinkles. Refrigerate until set, about 30 minutes.

White chocolate scorches more easily than dark chocolate, so keep an eye on it as it melts and microwave it in short (15-second) intervals.

Be sure to use canned pure pumpkin for these cookies and not pumpkin pie filling, which is sweetened.

Pumpkin Spice Latte Whoopie Pies

ACTIVE: 1 hr I TOTAL: 1 hr 35 min (plus cooling) I MAKES: about 24

FOR THE COOKIES

- 2 cups all-purpose flour
- 1 tablespoon pumpkin pie spice
- 1 teaspoon baking powder
- ½ teaspoon baking soda
- ½ teaspoon salt
- 6 tablespoons unsalted butter, at room temperature
- ¾ cup granulated sugar
- ½ cup packed light brown sugar
- ½ teaspoon pure vanilla extract
- 1 large egg, at room temperature
- 1 cup pure pumpkin puree

FOR THE FILLING

- 2 tablespoons milk
- 2 teaspoons instant coffee granules
- 1½ sticks (12 tablespoons) unsalted butter, at room temperature
- 1½ cups confectioners' sugar
- ¼ teaspoon salt
- Nonpareils, for decorating

1 Make the cookies: Position racks in the upper and lower thirds of the oven; preheat to 375°. Line 2 baking sheets with parchment paper. Whisk together the flour, pumpkin pie spice, baking powder, baking soda and salt in a bowl.

2 Beat the butter, granulated sugar, brown sugar and vanilla in a large bowl with a mixer on medium-high speed until pale and fluffy, about 5 minutes. Beat in the egg to combine. Reduce the mixer speed to low and beat in the pumpkin puree, scraping the bowl as needed. Beat in the flour mixture until just combined, 30 seconds to 1 minute.

3 Scoop mounds of batter (about 1½ tablespoons each) about 2 inches apart on the prepared baking sheets; shape into rounds with damp fingers. (Or you can transfer the batter to a piping bag fitted with a ½-inch round tip and pipe into 1½-inch rounds.) Bake, switching the pans halfway through, until the cookies are golden and the tops spring back when gently pressed, 14 to 16 minutes. Let the cookies cool 5 minutes on the pans, then carefully transfer to racks to cool completely. Repeat with the remaining batter.

4 Meanwhile, make the filling: Stir the milk and instant coffee in a small bowl until the coffee dissolves. Beat the butter, confectioners' sugar and salt in a large bowl with a mixer on low speed until combined, then increase the mixer speed to medium-high and beat until light and smooth, 3 minutes. Reduce the mixer speed to medium-low and beat in the milk mixture, scraping the bowl as needed, until smooth, 1 minute. Refrigerate until slightly firm, about 20 minutes.

5 Gently sandwich the filling (1 tablespoon per sandwich) between the flat sides of the cookies. Roll the edges in nonpareils. If the filling is soft, refrigerate the whoopie pies about 30 minutes, then let sit at room temperature before serving.

Plum Pie Cookies

ACTIVE: 1 hr **I** TOTAL: 2½ hr (plus cooling) **I** MAKES: about 18

2½ cups plus 1 tablespoon
    all-purpose flour

1   cup granulated sugar

¾   teaspoon salt

2   sticks unsalted butter,
    cut into cubes,
    at room temperature

1   large egg, lightly beaten,
    plus 1 beaten egg
    for brushing

½   teaspoon ground
    cinnamon

2   small plums

Turbinado sugar, for sprinkling

> **Cut a few slits in the top of each cookie, just like you would for a full-size pie. This allows steam to escape.**

1 Pulse 2½ cups flour, ½ cup granulated sugar and the salt in a food processor until combined. Add the butter and pulse until the mixture looks crumbly. Drizzle in 1 beaten egg and pulse until the dough holds together when pinched. Turn out onto a clean surface and knead a few times until the dough comes together. Divide the dough into 2 balls and place each ball on a separate piece of parchment paper. Top each with another piece of parchment and roll into two 11- to 12-inch rounds (about ⅛ inch thick). Refrigerate until firm, about 1 hour.

2 Position racks in the upper and lower thirds of the oven; preheat to 375°. Line 2 baking sheets with parchment paper. Whisk together the remaining ½ cup granulated sugar, 1 tablespoon flour and the cinnamon in a medium bowl. Halve, pit and thinly slice the plums, then cut each slice in half crosswise.

3 Cut out small rounds as close together as possible from 1 piece of dough using a 2½-inch round cookie cutter. Gather the scraps and refrigerate until firm; reroll once to cut out more rounds. Meanwhile, arrange 9 rounds on one of the baking sheets and brush the edges with some of the remaining beaten egg. Toss the plums in the cinnamon-sugar mixture to coat, then arrange about 4 plum pieces in the center of each dough round on the baking sheet, leaving space around the edges. Top each with a second round of dough and press the edges to seal. (If the dough is too stiff to work with, warm it briefly between your hands to make it more pliable.) Crimp the edges with a fork and cut 4 small steam vents into the top of each cookie. Transfer to the freezer and repeat with the remaining dough and plums.

4 Lightly brush the cookies with the remaining beaten egg and sprinkle with turbinado sugar. Bake, switching the pans halfway through, until the cookies are golden brown, 22 to 25 minutes. Let cool completely on the pans.

Strawberry Macarons

ACTIVE: 1 hr **I** TOTAL: 2½ hr (plus cooling) **I** MAKES: about 24

FOR THE MACARONS

3   large egg whites

1½ cups confectioners' sugar

¾   cup whole blanched
    almonds

2   pinches of kosher salt

3   tablespoons superfine
    sugar

¼   teaspoon strawberry
    extract

5   drops pink gel food
    coloring

FOR THE FILLING

1½ cups chopped hulled
    strawberries

2   tablespoons honey

1   tablespoon fresh lemon
    juice

A silicone mat is best for macarons. The cookies hold their shape better and bake more evenly than they do on parchment paper.

1 Make the macarons: Let the egg whites sit at room temperature for at least 1 hour. Line 2 baking sheets with silicone baking mats.

2 Pulse the confectioners' sugar and almonds in a food processor until finely ground. Working in batches, sift the mixture through a sieve into a large bowl. If you have more than 2 tablespoons of the mixture left in the sieve, return to the food processor and grind until powdery, then sift again.

3 Rub a pinch of salt around a large bowl or the bowl of a mixer to absorb any oils, then wipe clean. Add the egg whites and another pinch of salt and whisk with a mixer on medium speed until frothy. Gradually whisk in the superfine sugar, then whisk on medium-high speed until very soft peaks form, 2 to 4 minutes. Whisk in the strawberry extract and food coloring until stiff peaks form, 1 minute. Fold about one-third of the almond mixture into the egg whites, then fold in the rest. The batter should fall off the spatula in thick shiny ribbons. If the batter seems stiff, fold once or twice more, being careful not to overmix.

4 Transfer the batter to a piping bag fitted with a ¼-inch round tip. Holding the bag vertically and close to the prepared baking sheets, squeeze the bag until the batter spreads to a 1¼- to 1½-inch round, flicking your wrist to the side as you finish to avoid leaving a point. Repeat to make about 24 rounds per baking sheet, about 1½ inches apart. Firmly tap the baking sheets against the counter to release any air bubbles. Let sit at room temperature until the tops are slightly matte and no longer sticky, at least 45 minutes.

5 Meanwhile, preheat the oven to 325°. Make the filling: Bring the strawberries, honey and lemon juice to a simmer in a saucepan over medium heat. Cook, stirring and smashing the berries, until jammy, 20 to 25 minutes. Let cool.

6 Bake the macarons, 1 pan at a time, until risen and firm, 18 to 24 minutes. Let cool 10 minutes on the pan, then transfer to racks to cool completely. Sandwich a thin layer of the strawberry filling between the flat sides of the macarons.

Ginger-Maple Biscotti

ACTIVE: 45 min **I** TOTAL: 2 hr (plus cooling) **I** MAKES: about 20

FOR THE BISCOTTI

2   cups all-purpose flour

1½ teaspoons baking powder

1   tablespoon ground ginger

1   teaspoon ground cinnamon

½   teaspoon freshly grated nutmeg

6   tablespoons unsalted butter, at room temperature

¾   cup granulated pure maple sugar

¼   teaspoon salt

2   large eggs

1   teaspoon pure vanilla extract

1   cup crystallized ginger, finely chopped

FOR THE GLAZE

2   cups confectioners' sugar

2   tablespoons pure maple syrup

1   teaspoon maple extract

½   teaspoon ground ginger

2 to 3 tablespoons whole milk

Sprinkles, for decorating

1 Make the biscotti: Preheat the oven to 350° and line a baking sheet with parchment paper. Whisk together the flour, baking powder, ground ginger, cinnamon and nutmeg in a medium bowl.

2 In a large bowl, beat the butter, maple sugar and salt with a mixer on medium-high speed until light and fluffy, about 3 minutes. Beat in the eggs, one at a time, then the vanilla extract (it's OK if the mixture looks curdled). Add the flour mixture and beat on low speed until just combined. Stir in the crystallized ginger.

3 Scrape the dough into the middle of the baking sheet and gently press and shape with your hands into a 3-by-13-inch log. Bake until lightly browned on the top and sides and firm to the touch, 35 to 40 minutes. Let cool 30 minutes on the baking sheet, then remove the log to a cutting board, reserving the baking sheet and parchment.

4 Using a serrated knife, slice the log on the diagonal into ½- to ¾-inch-thick slices. Arrange the slices on the baking sheet, cut-side down. Bake until the tops of the biscotti are dry and browned, 20 minutes. Transfer to a rack to cool completely.

5 Make the glaze: Whisk together the confectioners' sugar, maple syrup, maple extract, ground ginger and 2 tablespoons milk in a medium bowl until smooth. Gradually whisk in up to 1 more tablespoon milk until the glaze is a dippable consistency. Dip each biscotti halfway into the glaze, letting the excess drip off, then return to the rack. Top with sprinkles. Let set, about 10 minutes.

These cookies have a triple dose of maple flavor: They're made with maple sugar, maple syrup and maple extract!

Chai Meringue Drops

ACTIVE: 35 min I TOTAL: 4 hr (plus cooling) I MAKES: about 60

1   bag English Breakfast tea
     (or about 1¼ teaspoons
     tea leaves)
½   teaspoon ground cardamom
¼   teaspoon ground cinnamon
¼   teaspoon ground ginger
¼   teaspoon ground cloves
3   large egg whites, at room
     temperature
¼   teaspoon cream of tartar
¼   teaspoon salt
¾   cup granulated sugar
1   teaspoon pure vanilla extract
White sanding sugar, for
     sprinkling

**The finer
the tea leaves,
the better. If yours
are large or coarse,
be sure to grind
them in a spice
grinder.**

1 Position racks in the upper and lower thirds of the oven; preheat to 225°. Line 2 baking sheets with parchment paper. Remove the tea leaves from the tea bag. If the leaves are large, finely grind them in a spice grinder. Mix the tea with the cardamom, cinnamon, ginger and cloves in a small bowl.

2 Whisk the egg whites in a large bowl with a mixer on medium speed until frothy, about 30 seconds. Beat in the cream of tartar and salt until soft peaks form, 3 to 4 minutes. Increase the mixer speed to medium-high and beat in the granulated sugar, 1 tablespoon at a time. Beat until stiff peaks form, 4 to 5 minutes. Beat in the vanilla and tea-spice mixture.

3 Transfer the meringue to a piping bag fitted with a ½-inch star tip. Pipe 1¼-inch mounds about 1 inch apart on the prepared pans. Sprinkle with sanding sugar. Bake, switching the pans halfway through, until the meringues are dry enough to peel off the parchment easily, about 2 hours. Turn off the oven; leave the meringues in the oven to finish drying, about 1 more hour. Let cool completely on the pans.

Cinnamon-Almond Melt-Aways

ACTIVE: 40 min **I** TOTAL: 2 hr (plus cooling) **I** MAKES: 48

¾ cup skin-on almonds

1¼ cups all-purpose flour

¼ cup rice flour

2 teaspoons ground cinnamon

¼ teaspoon salt

1¾ sticks (14 tablespoons) unsalted butter, at room temperature

1½ cups confectioners' sugar

2 teaspoons pure vanilla extract

> Melt-away cookies are made with a shortbread-like dough, so you don't need any eggs or leaveners for this recipe.

1 Position racks in the upper and lower thirds of the oven; preheat to 350°. Spread the almonds on a baking sheet and bake on the lower rack until toasted and lightly browned on the inside, 15 to 18 minutes. Let cool completely, then pulse in a food processor until very finely ground (do not grind to a paste). Add the all-purpose flour, rice flour, 1 teaspoon cinnamon and the salt. Pulse until combined.

2 Line 2 baking sheets with parchment paper. Beat the butter and ½ cup confectioners' sugar in a large bowl with a mixer on medium-high speed until pale and fluffy, about 3 minutes. Beat in the vanilla until combined. Reduce the mixer speed to low and beat in the flour mixture. Turn out the dough onto a large sheet of plastic wrap, flatten into a rectangle and wrap. Refrigerate until firm, about 1 hour.

3 Roll out the dough between 2 sheets of plastic wrap into an 8-by-9-inch rectangle (about ⅓ inch thick). If the dough starts to crack around the edges, pinch it back together with your fingers. Peel off the plastic wrap. With a short side facing you, slice the dough lengthwise into eight 1-inch-wide strips, then slice the strips crosswise into forty-eight 1½-inch rectangles (if the dough becomes too soft, refrigerate 15 minutes). Arrange the rectangles 1 inch apart on the pans.

4 Bake, switching the pans halfway through, until the cookies are set around the edges, 16 to 20 minutes. Let cool 5 minutes on the pans.

5 Meanwhile, whisk the remaining 1 cup confectioners' sugar and 1 teaspoon cinnamon in a shallow bowl. Gently toss the warm cookies in the sugar mixture to coat, then transfer to racks to cool completely. Toss the cooled cookies in the sugar mixture again.

Brownies & Bars

Classic Lemon Bars

ACTIVE: 30 min ❙ TOTAL: 1½ hr (plus 2 hr chilling) ❙ MAKES: about 24

FOR THE CRUST

Cooking spray

1½ sticks (12 tablespoons) cold unsalted butter, diced

2 cups all-purpose flour

¼ cup packed light brown sugar

¼ cup confectioners' sugar, plus more for dusting

¼ teaspoon salt

FOR THE FILLING

4 large eggs plus 2 egg yolks

2 cups granulated sugar

⅓ cup all-purpose flour, sifted

1 teaspoon grated lemon zest, plus 1 cup fresh lemon juice (from about 8 lemons)

Bring lemons to room temperature before you squeeze them so they'll yield more juice.

1 Make the crust: Preheat the oven to 350°. Line a 9-by-13-inch baking dish with foil, leaving a 2-inch overhang on all sides; spray the foil with cooking spray.

2 Pulse the butter, flour, brown sugar, confectioners' sugar and salt in a food processor until the dough comes together, about 1 minute. Press evenly into the bottom and about ½ inch up the sides of the baking dish, making sure there are no cracks. Bake until the crust is golden, about 25 minutes.

3 Meanwhile, make the filling: Whisk the whole eggs and yolks, granulated sugar and flour in a bowl until smooth. Whisk in the lemon zest and juice. Remove the crust from the oven and reduce the temperature to 300°. Pour the filling over the warm crust and return to the oven. Bake until the filling is just set, 30 to 35 minutes.

4 Transfer to a rack and let the bars cool completely in the pan, then refrigerate until firm, at least 2 hours. Lift out of the pan using the foil overhang; discard the foil. Cut into squares and dust with confectioners' sugar before serving.

Frosted Coffee Brownies

ACTIVE: 30 min **I** TOTAL: 1 hr (plus cooling) **I** MAKES: 12 to 16

FOR THE BROWNIES

Cooking spray

2 sticks unsalted butter

4 ounces semisweet chocolate, chopped

2 cups granulated sugar

3 tablespoons instant espresso powder

4 large eggs

1½ cups all-purpose flour

⅓ cup unsweetened cocoa powder

½ teaspoon salt

FOR THE FROSTING

1 tablespoon instant espresso powder

1 tablespoon milk

1 stick unsalted butter, at room temperature

¼ teaspoon salt

1½ cups confectioners' sugar

1 Make the brownies: Preheat the oven to 350°. Line a 9-by-13-inch baking dish with foil, leaving a 2-inch overhang on the long sides; coat the foil with cooking spray.

2 Melt the butter and chocolate in a medium saucepan over medium heat. Remove the pan from the heat and whisk in the granulated sugar, espresso powder and eggs until smooth. Stir in the flour, cocoa powder and salt.

3 Pour the batter into the baking dish and bake until a toothpick inserted into the center comes out clean, 30 to 35 minutes. Transfer to a rack and let cool completely in the pan. Lift the brownies out of the pan using the foil overhang; discard the foil.

4 Meanwhile, make the frosting: Combine the espresso powder and milk in a small bowl. In a medium bowl, beat the butter and salt with a mixer on medium-high speed until fluffy, about 2 minutes. Reduce the speed to low and gradually beat in the confectioners' sugar and milk mixture. Increase the speed to medium-high and beat until fluffy. Spread the frosting on the cooled brownies and cut into squares.

Instant espresso powder gives these brownies their intense coffee flavor. If you're sharing them with kids, make sure you use decaf!

Don't second-guess the beer! The brown ale gives these brownies an extra-rich caramel-like flavor.

Beer-Spiked Brownies with Pecan Icing

ACTIVE: 30 min | TOTAL: 1½ hr (plus cooling) | MAKES: 12 to 16

FOR THE BROWNIES
Cooking spray
1   12-ounce bottle brown ale
2   sticks unsalted butter
4   ounces semisweet chocolate, chopped
2   cups granulated sugar
4   large eggs
1½ cups all-purpose flour
⅓   cup unsweetened cocoa powder
½   teaspoon salt
1   cup semisweet chocolate chips

FOR THE GLAZE AND ICING
¼   cup plus 2 tablespoons brown ale
Pinch of granulated sugar
1   stick unsalted butter
1   cup finely chopped pecans
Pinch of salt
2   tablespoons unsweetened cocoa powder
2   cups confectioners' sugar

1 Make the brownies: Preheat the oven to 350°. Line a 9-by-13-inch baking dish with foil, leaving a 2-inch overhang on the short sides; coat the foil with cooking spray. Bring the ale to a simmer in a large saucepan over medium heat and cook until reduced to about ⅓ cup, about 15 minutes. Pour into a bowl and set aside.

2 Wipe out the saucepan and add the butter and chopped chocolate. Cook over medium-low heat, stirring, until smooth. Remove from the heat and let cool slightly, about 5 minutes. Add the granulated sugar and eggs and stir until glossy and smooth. Stir in the reduced ale. Add the flour, cocoa powder and salt and stir until no lumps remain. Stir in the chocolate chips.

3 Pour the batter into the baking dish. Bake until a toothpick inserted into the center comes out clean, 30 to 35 minutes. Transfer to a rack.

4 Meanwhile, make the glaze: Mix 2 tablespoons ale with the granulated sugar in a small bowl until the sugar is dissolved. Spoon or brush over the warm brownies and set aside.

5 Make the icing: Combine the butter, all but 2 tablespoons pecans and the salt in a medium saucepan over medium heat. Cook, stirring, until the butter is melted and the nuts are toasted, about 5 minutes. Add the cocoa powder and stir until smooth. Remove from the heat and add the confectioners' sugar in 2 batches, alternating with the remaining ¼ cup ale. Stir until smooth.

6 Pour the icing over the warm brownies and gently spread. Sprinkle with the remaining 2 tablespoons pecans. Let cool completely. Lift the brownies out of the pan using the foil overhang; discard the foil. Cut into squares.

Salted Pretzel Marshmallow Bars

ACTIVE: 30 min I TOTAL: 1 hr (plus cooling) I MAKES: 16

FOR THE BARS

Cooking spray

1½ cups broken pretzel pieces

1¼ cups all-purpose flour

1½ teaspoons baking powder

1 teaspoon kosher salt

1 stick unsalted butter

1½ cups packed light brown sugar

2 large eggs, lightly beaten

2 teaspoons pure vanilla extract

FOR THE TOPPING

8 marshmallows, halved crosswise

¼ cup peanut butter chips

1 teaspoon vegetable oil

¼ cup semisweet chocolate chips

> Arrange the marshmallows on top of the bars in a 4-by-4 grid so you get one on every piece.

1 Make the bars: Preheat the oven to 350˚. Line a 9-inch square baking pan with foil, leaving a 2-inch overhang on all sides. Lightly spray the foil with cooking spray.

2 Pulse 1 cup pretzel pieces in a food processor until finely ground (you should have about ½ cup crumbs). Transfer to a bowl. Whisk in the flour, baking powder and salt.

3 Melt the butter in a saucepan over medium heat. Remove from the heat and stir in the brown sugar. Let cool slightly, then stir in the eggs and vanilla. Stir the pretzel crumb mixture into the butter mixture in 2 additions.

4 Spread the batter in the prepared pan. Scatter the remaining ½ cup pretzel pieces on top. Bake until golden and a toothpick inserted into the center comes out clean with a few crumbs, 25 to 30 minutes. Transfer to a rack and let cool completely in the pan. Lift the bars out of the pan using the foil overhang; discard the foil. Transfer the bars to a baking sheet.

5 Make the topping: Preheat the broiler. Press the marshmallow halves, cut-side down, in even rows on top of the bars. Broil, rotating the baking sheet as needed, until the marshmallows are golden brown, 1 to 2 minutes. Let cool on the pan.

6 Put the peanut butter chips and ½ teaspoon vegetable oil in a microwave-safe bowl and microwave in 30-second intervals, stirring, until melted and smooth. Repeat with the chocolate chips and the remaining ½ teaspoon vegetable oil in another bowl. Drizzle the melted peanut butter and chocolate mixtures over the bars. Let harden at room temperature or refrigerate to set before cutting.

Be sure to use cream of coconut, which is sweet and syrupy, for these bars and not coconut milk or coconut cream.

Piña Colada Cheesecake Bars

ACTIVE: 45 min | TOTAL: 4½ hr (plus overnight chilling) | MAKES: about 12

FOR THE CRUST

3   tablespoons unsalted butter, melted, plus more for the pan

16 to 18 shortbread cookies, finely ground (about 1 cup)

1   tablespoon sugar

FOR THE FILLING

2   8-ounce packages cream cheese, at room temperature

⅓   cup cream of coconut

⅓   cup sugar

Pinch of salt

2   large eggs, at room temperature

¼   cup sour cream

1   teaspoon coconut extract

FOR THE TOPPING

1   cup chopped dried pineapple

1   8-ounce can crushed pineapple in juice

2   tablespoons cream of coconut

1   tablespoon fresh lemon juice

⅔   cup water

1 Make the crust: Preheat the oven to 350°. Line an 8-inch square baking dish with foil, leaving a 2-inch overhang on 2 sides; lightly brush with melted butter. Toss together the cookie crumbs, sugar and melted butter in a small bowl until well combined. Firmly press the mixture evenly into the bottom of the pan to make a thin layer. Bake until firm and lightly browned, about 10 minutes. Let cool at least 20 minutes. Reduce the oven temperature to 325°.

2 Make the filling: Beat the cream cheese, cream of coconut, sugar and salt in a large bowl with a mixer on medium-high speed, scraping down the bowl a few times, until smooth and fluffy, 3 to 5 minutes. Reduce the mixer speed to medium; beat in the eggs, sour cream and coconut extract until combined. Spread the filling over the crust.

3 Bake until the edges are set but the center is still a little jiggly, 35 to 45 minutes. Transfer to a rack and let cool to room temperature, about 3 hours.

4 Meanwhile, make the topping: Combine the dried and crushed pineapple, cream of coconut, lemon juice and water in a small saucepan over medium-high heat. Bring to a simmer, stirring, then reduce the heat to medium-low and cook, stirring occasionally, until the dried pineapple is tender and the liquid has reduced to just a few spoonfuls of syrup, about 20 minutes. Let cool, stirring occasionally, 30 to 45 minutes.

5 Spoon the topping over the cheesecake layer and gently spread to cover. Cover with plastic wrap and refrigerate overnight.

6 Lift the bars out of the pan using the foil overhang; discard the foil. Cut into squares.

For clean cuts,
run your knife
under hot water
and wipe dry
before slicing.

Snickerdoodle Ice Cream Sandwiches

ACTIVE: 40 min ▮ TOTAL: 1 hr 55 min (plus 4 hr freezing) ▮ MAKES: 12 to 15

2¼ cups all-purpose flour

1½ teaspoons cream of tartar

1 teaspoon baking soda

1 teaspoon salt

2 sticks unsalted butter, at room temperature

1¼ cups granulated sugar

¼ cup packed light brown sugar

2 large eggs

2 teaspoons pure vanilla extract

1 tablespoon ground cinnamon

3 pints dulce de leche or vanilla bean ice cream, or a combination

1 Preheat the oven to 400°. Line a 13-by-18-inch rimmed baking sheet with parchment paper. Whisk the flour, cream of tartar, baking soda and salt in a medium bowl.

2 Beat the butter, 1 cup granulated sugar and the brown sugar in a large bowl with a mixer on medium-high speed until light and fluffy, about 4 minutes. Beat in the eggs and vanilla. Reduce the mixer speed to low and slowly beat in the flour mixture. Increase the speed to medium-high and beat briefly until combined.

3 Scrape the dough onto the baking sheet; spread evenly into a 10-by-13-inch rectangle using a rubber spatula. Combine the remaining ¼ cup granulated sugar and the cinnamon in a small bowl; sprinkle over the dough. Bake until golden around the edges, cracked on top and the center is just set but still soft, 10 to 12 minutes. (Do not overbake; the cookie will firm up as it cools.) Transfer to a rack and let cool completely in the pan, about 1 hour. Cut in half crosswise.

4 Remove the ice cream from the freezer and let soften, about 15 minutes. Line a 9-by-13-inch baking dish with plastic wrap, leaving a 4-inch overhang on all sides. Put 1 cookie half in the baking dish, cinnamon sugar–side down. Scoop the softened ice cream on top, covering it completely. Spread the ice cream gently with an offset spatula into an even layer, filling in any gaps or air pockets. Top with the other cookie half, cinnamon sugar–side up. Wrap tightly with the overhanging plastic wrap. Freeze in the pan until the ice cream is very firm, about 4 hours.

5 Carefully lift the whole sandwich from the baking dish and remove the plastic wrap. Using a sharp knife, trim the edges, then cut into bars.

Key Lime Pie Macaroon Bars

ACTIVE: 30 min **I** TOTAL: 1 hr 20 min (plus 5 hr cooling and chilling) **I** MAKES: about 30

FOR THE CRUST

Cooking spray

2 cups finely ground graham cracker crumbs (from about 18 crackers)

3 tablespoons granulated sugar

1 stick unsalted butter, melted

FOR THE FILLING AND TOPPING

1 14-ounce can sweetened condensed milk

½ cup bottled Key lime juice

1 teaspoon finely grated lime zest, plus more for topping

½ teaspoon pure vanilla extract

⅛ teaspoon salt

1 14-ounce bag sweetened shredded coconut

½ cup heavy cream

1 tablespoon confectioners' sugar

1 Make the crust: Preheat the oven to 325°. Line an 8-inch square baking dish with foil; coat the foil with cooking spray. Combine the graham cracker crumbs and granulated sugar in a medium bowl, then stir in the melted butter until the mixture is the consistency of wet sand. Press firmly and evenly into the bottom of the baking dish. Bake until the crust is light golden brown, 10 to 15 minutes. Let cool.

2 Make the filling: Whisk together the condensed milk, Key lime juice, lime zest, vanilla and salt in a bowl until smooth. Stir in the coconut. Spread the coconut mixture over the cooled crust. Bake until golden around the edges, about 30 minutes. Let cool to room temperature, about 1 hour, then refrigerate until chilled, 3 to 4 hours. Cut into small squares.

3 Make the topping: Combine the heavy cream and confectioners' sugar in a medium bowl and beat with a mixer on medium-high speed or whisk by hand until stiff peaks form. Transfer to a piping bag fitted with a star tip; pipe onto the macaroon bars. Top with lime zest. Refrigerate until ready to serve.

Key limes taste slightly more tart and floral than regular limes. They're hard to juice, so look for the bottled version, or just use regular lime juice!

Air-Fryer Pecan Brownies

ACTIVE: 20 min I TOTAL: 1 hr 10 min I MAKES: about 8

Cooking spray

1 stick unsalted butter

4 ounces bittersweet chocolate, chopped

½ cup all-purpose flour

6 tablespoons unsweetened cocoa powder

½ teaspoon salt

1 cup sugar

2 large eggs

1 teaspoon pure vanilla extract

¾ cup toasted pecans, coarsely chopped

Vanilla ice cream, for serving

1 Coat an 8-inch round cake pan with cooking spray. Line with 2 strips of overhanging parchment paper.

2 Combine the butter and chocolate in a heatproof bowl set over a saucepan filled with a few inches of simmering water (do not let the bowl touch the water). Cook, stirring, until melted. Remove the bowl from the pan and let cool slightly. Stir together the flour, cocoa powder and salt in a bowl.

3 Whisk the sugar and eggs in a large bowl until light and creamy, about 1 minute. Whisk in the vanilla and the melted chocolate mixture, then mix in the flour mixture and pecans. Pour the batter into the cake pan.

4 Set the pan in a 6-quart air fryer. Air-fry at 320° until a toothpick inserted into the center comes out mostly clean, 18 to 20 minutes. Let cool on a rack 30 minutes, then remove the brownies from the pan using the parchment overhang; discard the parchment. Cut the brownies into wedges. Serve with ice cream.

An air fryer works like a mini convection oven. It's great for small-batch baking.

Strawberry-Walnut Blondies

ACTIVE: 20 min | TOTAL: 40 min (plus cooling) | MAKES: about 9

4   tablespoons unsalted butter, plus more for the pan

1   cup packed light brown sugar

1½   teaspoons pure vanilla extract

1   large egg, lightly beaten

¾   cup all-purpose flour

½   teaspoon salt

¼   teaspoon baking powder

¼   cup butterscotch chips

¼   cup chopped walnuts

3   tablespoons strawberry jam

1   Preheat the oven to 350°. Line an 8-inch square baking pan with foil, leaving an overhang on 2 sides. Butter the foil.

2   Combine the butter and brown sugar in a large microwave-safe bowl. Microwave until the butter is melted, about 1 minute. Stir in the vanilla. Let cool slightly, then stir in the egg.

3   Whisk the flour, salt and baking powder in a small bowl. Stir into the butter mixture. Stir in the butterscotch chips and walnuts and spread the batter in the pan. Drop dollops of jam on top and swirl with a knife.

4   Bake the blondies until set, 20 to 25 minutes. Transfer to a rack and let cool 15 minutes in the pan, then lift the blondies out of the pan using the foil and transfer to the rack to cool completely. Discard the foil and cut the blondies into squares.

This recipe is easy to customize: Just swap in your favorite nuts and jam. Try a combo of almonds and blueberry jam or pistachios and raspberry jam.

For the best flavor, use maple syrup that's labeled "dark" or "robust" in this recipe.

Maple-Walnut Blondies

ACTIVE: 45 min **I** TOTAL: 1 hr (plus cooling) **I** MAKES: 12 to 16

FOR THE BLONDIES

Cooking spray

1 cup walnuts

2¾ cups all-purpose flour

½ teaspoon baking soda

½ teaspoon kosher salt

2 sticks unsalted butter, chopped

1¼ cups packed light brown sugar

½ cup pure maple syrup

2 large eggs, at room temperature

1 teaspoon pure vanilla extract

1 teaspoon maple extract

FOR THE FROSTING

1½ sticks (12 tablespoons) unsalted butter, at room temperature

¼ teaspoon kosher salt

⅓ cup pure maple syrup (dark or robust)

1½ cups confectioners' sugar

1 teaspoon fresh lemon juice

¼ teaspoon maple extract, plus more to taste

1 Make the blondies: Preheat the oven to 350°. Line a 9-by-13-inch baking dish with foil, leaving a 2-inch overhang on the long sides; coat the foil with cooking spray. Spread the walnuts on a baking sheet and bake until lightly browned, 10 to 12 minutes. Let cool slightly, then transfer to a cutting board and roughly chop.

2 Whisk the flour, baking soda and salt in a large bowl. Melt the butter in a medium saucepan over medium heat and cook, stirring occasionally with a whisk, until brown flecks appear, 10 to 12 minutes. Remove from the heat and immediately whisk in the brown sugar and maple syrup. Let cool slightly, about 5 minutes. Whisk in the eggs one at a time, then add the vanilla and maple extracts. Whisk the brown butter–egg mixture into the flour mixture, then fold in the walnuts with a rubber spatula.

3 Spread the batter in the baking dish. Bake until lightly browned and a toothpick inserted into the center comes out clean, about 25 minutes. Transfer to a rack and let cool completely in the pan. Lift the blondies out of the pan using the foil overhang; discard the foil.

4 Meanwhile, make the frosting: Beat the butter and salt in a large bowl with a mixer on medium-high speed until fluffy, about 2 minutes. Add the maple syrup and beat until smooth. Gradually beat in the confectioners' sugar on low speed, increasing the speed to medium-high after each addition, until fluffy. Beat in the lemon juice and maple extract; add more maple extract, ¼ teaspoon at a time, to taste. Spread the frosting over the cooled blondies. Cut into squares.

Mochi Brownies

ACTIVE: 20 min **I** TOTAL: 1½ hr **I** MAKES: about 12

Cooking spray

1⅔ cups granulated sugar

1¼ cups mochiko (glutinous rice flour or sweet rice flour)

¾ cup unsweetened black cocoa powder

¾ teaspoon salt

½ teaspoon baking powder

2 sticks unsalted butter

1 cup milk

2 large eggs

2 teaspoons pure vanilla extract

Confectioners' sugar, for dusting

1 Preheat the oven to 350°. Line an 8-inch square baking dish with parchment paper, leaving a 2-inch overhang on 2 sides; coat with cooking spray.

2 Whisk the granulated sugar, mochiko, cocoa powder, salt and baking powder in a medium bowl until well combined and lump-free. Melt the butter in a medium saucepan over medium heat. Remove from the heat and let cool slightly. Add the milk, eggs and vanilla to the saucepan and whisk until smooth. Add the dry ingredients and whisk until blended.

3 Pour the batter into the baking dish. Bake until the edges are firm, the center is soft but not jiggly and a toothpick inserted into the center comes out clean or with a few crumbs, 1 hour to 1 hour 10 minutes. Transfer to a rack and let cool completely in the pan. Lift the brownies out of the pan using the parchment overhang; discard the parchment. Dust with confectioners' sugar and cut into squares.

These brownies are made with glutinous rice flour, which gives mochi that signature super-chewy texture. Bonus: They're gluten-free!

Dark Chocolate Pecan Bars

ACTIVE: 30 min **I** TOTAL: 1 hr 20 min (plus cooling) **I** MAKES: about 24

FOR THE CRUST

Cooking spray

⅓ cup pecans

2   cups all-purpose flour

½   cup granulated sugar

½   teaspoon salt

1½ sticks (12 tablespoons) cold unsalted butter, cut into cubes

FOR THE TOPPING

¾   cup dark corn syrup

½   cup granulated sugar

½   cup packed light brown sugar

4   large eggs

4   tablespoons unsalted butter, melted

2   teaspoons pure vanilla extract

Pinch of salt

1½ cups pecans, roughly chopped

3   ounces bittersweet chocolate, roughly chopped

1 Make the crust: Preheat the oven to 350°. Line a 9-by-13-inch baking dish with foil, leaving a 2-inch overhang on the long sides; coat the foil with cooking spray. Pulse the pecans in a food processor until finely ground. Add the flour, granulated sugar and salt and pulse to combine. Add the cold butter and pulse until the dough starts clumping together (it will still be crumbly). Transfer to the baking dish and press into an even layer with your fingers. Bake until golden brown and set, 25 to 30 minutes.

2 Meanwhile, make the topping: Whisk the corn syrup, granulated sugar, brown sugar, eggs, melted butter, vanilla and salt in a large bowl until smooth. Stir in the pecans.

3 Spread the topping over the warm crust and sprinkle evenly with the chocolate. Return to the oven and bake until the top is set and no longer jiggly, 25 to 30 minutes. Transfer to a rack and let cool completely in the pan. Lift the bars out of the pan using the foil overhang; discard the foil. Cut into diamonds or squares.

Dark and light corn syrup are generally interchangeable, but the dark stuff is especially good in this recipe: It has a rich molasses flavor.

Chocolate-Covered Shortbread

ACTIVE: 30 min **I** TOTAL: 1 hr 50 min (plus cooling) **I** MAKES: about 16

2   sticks unsalted butter, at room temperature, plus more for the pan

1½ cups all-purpose flour

½   cup whole-wheat flour

1   cup confectioners' sugar

½   teaspoon kosher salt

1   teaspoon pure vanilla extract

3   ounces semisweet chocolate, chopped

Silver nonpareils, for decorating

1 Preheat the oven to 300°. Lightly butter the bottom and sides of a 9-inch round fluted tart pan. Combine both flours, the confectioners' sugar and salt in a food processor and pulse until combined. Add the butter and vanilla; pulse until the flour is moistened and the dough just begins to clump.

2 Press the dough evenly into the tart pan. Prick the dough all over with a fork, about 30 times.

3 Bake until the shortbread is lightly golden and set in the center, 60 to 70 minutes. Transfer to a rack to cool 10 minutes in the pan, then sprinkle with the chopped chocolate. Let the chocolate soften, about 5 minutes, then spread into a thin layer with an offset spatula, leaving a ½-inch border around the edge. Top with nonpareils; let cool completely.

4 Remove the shortbread from the pan and transfer to a cutting board. Cut into wedges.

Make sure you prick the dough all over before you bake it. The holes let steam escape and keep the shortbread from puffing up.

Red Velvet
Cheesecake Brownies

ACTIVE: 35 min I TOTAL: 2½ hr (plus cooling) I MAKES: 16 to 24

FOR THE CHEESECAKE LAYER

Cooking spray

- 12 ounces cream cheese, at room temperature
- ⅓ cup sugar
- 1 large egg
- ½ teaspoon unsweetened dutch-process cocoa powder
- ¼ teaspoon red gel food coloring
- 1 tablespoon buttermilk

FOR THE BROWNIE LAYER

- 2 sticks unsalted butter
- 1¾ cups sugar
- 3 large eggs
- 1 teaspoon pure vanilla extract
- 1 cup all-purpose flour
- ¾ cup unsweetened dutch-process cocoa powder
- ¾ teaspoon salt
- ½ teaspoon baking powder

1 Make the cheesecake layer: Preheat the oven to 350°. Line a 9-by-13-inch baking pan with foil, leaving a 2-inch overhang on the short sides; coat the foil with cooking spray. Beat the cream cheese, sugar and egg in a medium bowl with a mixer on medium speed until smooth and fluffy, 2 to 3 minutes. Transfer ⅓ cup of the batter to a small bowl and stir in the cocoa powder and red food coloring until smooth; stir in the buttermilk. Set aside the 2 batters.

2 Make the brownie layer: Melt the butter in a medium saucepan over medium heat. Remove from the heat and let cool slightly. Stir in the sugar, eggs and vanilla until well combined. Stir in the flour, cocoa powder, salt and baking powder until smooth.

3 Spread the brownie batter in the pan. Top with small spoonfuls of the plain cheesecake batter so most of the brownie is covered. Spoon the red cheesecake batter on top; gently swirl the cheesecake batters together with a skewer.

4 Bake until a toothpick inserted into the center of the brownies comes out clean, 35 to 40 minutes. Transfer to a rack and let cool completely in the pan. Lift the bars out of the pan using the foil overhang; discard the foil. Cut into squares.

To get this vibrant red color, use gel food coloring. It's much more concentrated than the liquid kind, so you can use less.

Cupcakes

To get this swirled look, fill 2 piping bags with different kinds of frosting; flatten the bags slightly, then put them in another piping bag fitted with a star tip.

Chocolate Egg Cream Cupcakes

ACTIVE: 50 min **I** TOTAL: 1 hr 20 min (plus cooling) **I** MAKES: 6

FOR THE CUPCAKES

- ¼ cup unsweetened cocoa powder
- ⅓ cup hot water
- ¼ cup chocolate syrup
- ⅔ cup all-purpose flour
- ⅓ cup granulated sugar
- ¼ teaspoon baking soda
- ¼ teaspoon baking powder
- ¼ teaspoon salt
- ¼ cup vegetable oil
- 1 large egg
- 2 tablespoons whole milk
- ½ teaspoon pure vanilla extract

FOR THE FROSTING

- 1 ounce milk chocolate, chopped
- 6 tablespoons unsalted butter, cut into pieces, at room temperature
- ½ teaspoon pure vanilla extract
- 2 cups confectioners' sugar
- ¼ cup whole milk
- 2 tablespoons unsweetened cocoa powder
- 2 pinches of salt
- 2 tablespoons malted milk powder

Small pretzel rods, for topping

1. Make the cupcakes: Preheat the oven to 350°. Line a 6-cup muffin pan with cupcake liners. Whisk together the cocoa powder and hot water in a large bowl. Whisk in the chocolate syrup until smooth; let cool slightly. In another large bowl, whisk together the flour, granulated sugar, baking soda, baking powder and salt.

2. Whisk the vegetable oil, egg, milk and vanilla into the cocoa mixture until smooth, then fold into the flour mixture until just combined. Divide the batter among the muffin cups. Bake until a toothpick inserted into the center of a cupcake comes out clean, 18 to 20 minutes. Let cool 10 minutes in the pan, then transfer the cupcakes to a rack to cool completely.

3. Make the frosting: Put the chocolate in a microwave-safe bowl; microwave in 30-second intervals, stirring, until melted. Let cool slightly. In a large bowl, beat the butter, vanilla and confectioners' sugar with a mixer on medium-high speed until fluffy. Add 3 tablespoons milk; beat until smooth, about 3 minutes. Remove half of the frosting to a separate bowl; add the cocoa powder, melted chocolate and a pinch of salt and beat until fluffy, about 2 minutes. Mix together the remaining 1 tablespoon milk and the malted milk powder in a cup, then add to the plain frosting; add the remaining pinch of salt and beat until fluffy, about 2 minutes. If the frosting is too soft, cover and refrigerate until it is firm enough to pipe.

4. To decorate, put the two frostings in separate piping bags (or zip-top bags). Snip off the tips. Position side by side in another piping bag fitted with a large star tip. Pipe the frosting onto the cupcakes in a spiral motion to create a swirl. Top each cupcake with a pretzel rod.

To keep the candied bacon nice and crisp, garnish the cupcakes as close to serving time as possible.

Chocolate-Bacon Cupcakes with Dulce de Leche Frosting

ACTIVE: 45 min I TOTAL: 2 hr (plus cooling) I MAKES: 12

FOR THE CANDIED BACON

- ½ cup packed light brown sugar
- 2 tablespoons granulated sugar
- 2 teaspoons unsweetened dutch-process cocoa powder
- 12 slices bacon, cut in half

FOR THE CUPCAKES

- 5 tablespoons vegetable oil
- ¼ cup brewed espresso
- ¼ cup packed light brown sugar
- ⅓ cup unsweetened dutch-process cocoa powder
- 4 ounces milk chocolate, chopped
- ¾ cup all-purpose flour
- ½ cup granulated sugar
- ½ teaspoon baking soda
- ½ teaspoon fine salt
- ¼ cup buttermilk
- 2 large eggs
- 1 teaspoon pure vanilla extract

FOR THE FROSTING

- 1 cup jarred dulce de leche
- 8 ounces cream cheese, at room temperature
- 1 teaspoon pure vanilla extract

Flaky sea salt, for topping

1. Make the candied bacon: Preheat the oven to 350° and set a rack on a foil-lined baking sheet. Whisk together the brown sugar, granulated sugar and cocoa powder in a medium bowl. Toss the bacon in the sugar mixture until well coated, then arrange on the rack in a single layer. Bake until dark brown, 15 to 20 minutes. Let cool, then pat dry with paper towels. Chop 6 pieces of the bacon.

2. Meanwhile, make the cupcakes: Combine the vegetable oil, espresso, brown sugar, cocoa powder and chocolate in a large microwave-safe bowl and microwave until hot, about 2 minutes. Whisk until smooth, then let cool about 15 minutes.

3. Whisk together the flour, granulated sugar, baking soda and fine salt in a medium bowl. Add the buttermilk, eggs and vanilla to the cooled chocolate mixture and whisk until smooth. Add the flour mixture and whisk until combined.

4. Line a 12-cup muffin pan with cupcake liners. Divide the batter among the cups, then sprinkle with the chopped bacon. Bake until the cupcakes spring back when lightly pressed, 20 to 25 minutes. Let cool 10 minutes in the pan, then transfer the cupcakes to a rack to cool completely.

5. Meanwhile, make the frosting: Beat the dulce de leche, cream cheese and vanilla in a large bowl with a mixer on medium speed until combined. Transfer to a piping bag fitted with a large star tip; refrigerate 30 minutes.

6. Pipe the frosting onto the cupcakes. Top with the remaining candied bacon, breaking it into smaller pieces; sprinkle with flaky sea salt.

Squeeze your lemon juice through a fine-mesh sieve set over a bowl to catch any seeds or pulp.

Lemon Meringue Cupcakes

ACTIVE: 1 hr **I** TOTAL: 1½ hr (plus cooling) **I** MAKES: 12

FOR THE CUPCAKES

1¾ cups all-purpose flour

½ teaspoon baking powder

¼ teaspoon baking soda

¼ teaspoon salt

2 large eggs

1¾ cups granulated sugar

1 cup whole milk

¾ cup vegetable oil

Grated zest of 2 lemons, plus
    2 tablespoons lemon juice

1 teaspoon pure vanilla extract

FOR THE MERINGUE

2 large egg whites

¼ teaspoon salt

½ cup granulated sugar

½ cup light corn syrup

¼ cup water

¼ teaspoon pure vanilla extract

FOR THE GLAZE

2½ cups confectioners' sugar

¼ cup fresh lemon juice
    (from about 2 lemons)

1 tablespoon limoncello or
    other lemon-flavored liqueur
    (optional)

6 to 7 drops yellow food coloring
    (optional)

1. Make the cupcakes: Preheat the oven to 350°. Line a 12-cup muffin pan with cupcake liners. Whisk together the flour, baking powder, baking soda and salt in a medium bowl. Whisk together the eggs, granulated sugar, milk, vegetable oil, lemon zest, lemon juice and vanilla in another large bowl until combined. Whisk the flour mixture into the egg mixture until just combined.

2. Divide the batter among the muffin cups, filling them to just below the rim. Bake until a toothpick inserted into the center of a cupcake comes out clean, 25 to 30 minutes. Let cool 15 minutes in the pan, then transfer the cupcakes to a rack to cool completely.

3. Make the meringue: Beat the egg whites and salt in a large bowl with a mixer on medium speed until foamy, about 1 minute. Increase the speed to high and gradually beat in 2 tablespoons granulated sugar; beat until stiff peaks form, about 3 minutes.

4. Combine the remaining 6 tablespoons granulated sugar, the corn syrup and water in a saucepan over medium-high heat. Cook until the mixture registers 245° on a candy thermometer, about 6 minutes; remove from the heat. With the mixer on medium speed, slowly pour the hot sugar syrup into the egg whites; increase the speed to high and beat until the meringue is fluffy and cool, about 6 minutes. Beat in the vanilla. Transfer the meringue to a piping bag fitted with a large round tip and pipe onto the cupcakes; set aside at room temperature to firm up, about 15 minutes.

5. Meanwhile, make the glaze: Whisk together the confectioners' sugar, lemon juice, limoncello and food coloring (if using) in a microwave-safe bowl until smooth. Microwave 1 minute, then whisk again until the sugar dissolves; let cool about 5 minutes, stirring occasionally. Dip the meringue-covered tops of the cupcakes into the glaze, letting the excess drip off. If the glaze gets too thick, microwave 20 seconds. Let set.

We used silicone liners for these cupcakes. They come in tons of fun colors and they're easy to clean and reuse!

Orange Cream Cupcakes

ACTIVE: 1 hr ∎ TOTAL: 1½ hr (plus cooling) ∎ MAKES: 12

FOR THE CUPCAKES

1½ cups all-purpose flour

1½ teaspoons baking powder

¼ teaspoon salt

2 large eggs, at room temperature

⅔ cup granulated sugar

1½ sticks (12 tablespoons) unsalted butter, melted

2 teaspoons finely grated orange zest

1 teaspoon pure vanilla extract

½ cup whole milk

FOR THE FROSTING

2 teaspoons finely grated orange zest, plus ¾ cup orange juice (from about 2 oranges)

1 8-ounce package cream cheese, at room temperature

1¼ sticks (10 tablespoons) unsalted butter, cut into pieces, at room temperature

1 cup confectioners' sugar

½ teaspoon pure vanilla extract

3 drops yellow food coloring (optional)

1 drop red food coloring (optional)

Candied orange zest, for topping

1 Make the cupcakes: Preheat the oven to 350°. Line a 12-cup muffin pan with cupcake liners. Whisk together the flour, baking powder and salt in a medium bowl.

2 Beat the eggs and granulated sugar in a large bowl with a mixer on medium-high speed until pale and fluffy, about 2 minutes. Reduce the mixer speed to medium-low and slowly pour in the melted butter, then add the orange zest and vanilla, beating until fully combined. Beat in the flour mixture in 2 additions, alternating with the milk, beginning and ending with the flour mixture, until just combined (do not overmix).

3 Divide the batter among the muffin cups, filling each about two-thirds of the way. Bake until a toothpick inserted into the center of a cupcake comes out clean, about 18 minutes. Let cool 5 minutes in the pan, then transfer the cupcakes to a rack to cool completely.

4 Meanwhile, make the frosting: Bring the orange juice to a boil in a saucepan. Reduce the heat to medium and simmer until reduced to 1½ tablespoons, about 8 minutes. Let cool.

5 Beat the cream cheese in a large bowl with a mixer on medium-high speed until smooth and fluffy. Beat in the butter, a little at a time, until smooth. Reduce the mixer speed to low; sift the confectioners' sugar into the bowl and beat until smooth. Add the vanilla, the cooled orange syrup, orange zest and food coloring; beat on medium speed until combined. Refrigerate until spreadable, about 15 minutes. Spread the frosting on the cupcakes; top with candied orange zest.

You don't need fancy tools to shave chocolate: Just use a vegetable peeler!

Chocolate Ganache Cupcakes

ACTIVE: 1 hr | TOTAL: 1½ hr (plus cooling) | MAKES: 12

FOR THE CUPCAKES

- 3 tablespoons unsweetened cocoa powder (not dutch-process)
- ¼ cup water
- 2 ounces unsweetened chocolate, chopped
- 1 cup all-purpose flour
- ½ teaspoon baking soda
- ⅛ teaspoon kosher salt
- 6 tablespoons unsalted butter, at room temperature
- 1 cup granulated sugar
- 2 large eggs
- ⅓ cup whole milk
- 1 tablespoon orange-flavored liqueur, rum or brandy (optional)

FOR THE GANACHE

- 10 ounces semisweet chocolate, chopped
- 1⅓ cups heavy cream
- Pinch of kosher salt
- 1 tablespoon confectioners' sugar
- Shaved white chocolate, for topping

1. Make the cupcakes: Preheat the oven to 350°. Line a 12-cup muffin pan with cupcake liners. Stir together the cocoa powder and water in a small bowl until smooth. Put the unsweetened chocolate in a microwave-safe bowl and microwave in 30-second intervals, stirring, until melted; let cool.

2. Sift the flour and baking soda into a large bowl; stir in the salt. Beat the butter and granulated sugar in another large bowl with a mixer on medium speed until smooth. Beat in the eggs, one at a time, until combined. Reduce the mixer speed to low and add the cocoa mixture and melted chocolate; mix until combined. Beat in the flour mixture in 2 batches, alternating with the milk, beginning and ending with the flour, until combined. Beat in the liqueur (if using).

3. Divide the batter among the muffin cups, filling them three-quarters of the way. Bake until a toothpick inserted into the center of a cupcake comes out clean, 20 to 25 minutes. Let cool 10 minutes in the pan, then transfer the cupcakes to a rack to cool completely.

4. Meanwhile, make the ganache: Combine the semisweet chocolate, 1 cup heavy cream and the salt in a heatproof bowl set over a pan of simmering water (do not let the bowl touch the water); stir until melted and smooth, about 8 minutes. Remove the bowl from the saucepan and set aside until the ganache is cool and thick (but not hard), about 1 hour.

5. Beat the remaining ⅓ cup heavy cream and the confectioners' sugar in a large bowl with a mixer on medium speed until soft peaks form. Fold in ¼ cup of the cooled ganache. Cut a small hole (about ½ inch deep) into the center of each cupcake with a paring knife; remove the cake. Use a small spoon to fill the hole with the chocolate whipped cream.

6. Beat the remaining ganache with a mixer on medium speed until light and fluffy, 3 to 5 minutes. (Be careful not to overmix or the ganache will become grainy.) Transfer the whipped ganache to a piping bag fitted with a star tip and pipe onto the cupcakes. Top with shaved white chocolate.

We put vanilla wafer crumbs and banana in the batter to get that classic banana pudding flavor!

Banana Pudding Cupcakes

ACTIVE: 1 hr **|** TOTAL: 1½ hr (plus cooling) **|** MAKES: 12

FOR THE CUPCAKES AND FILLING

- 1 cup all-purpose flour
- ⅔ cup finely ground vanilla wafer cookies (from about ¾ cup whole cookies)
- 1¼ teaspoons baking powder
- ½ teaspoon salt
- 1½ sticks (12 tablespoons) unsalted butter, at room temperature
- ½ cup granulated sugar
- 2 large eggs, at room temperature
- ½ cup milk, at room temperature
- 2 teaspoons pure vanilla extract
- 1 large banana, peeled and finely chopped
- ½ cup white chocolate chips
- ¼ cup heavy cream

FOR THE FROSTING

- 2 sticks unsalted butter, at room temperature
- Pinch of salt
- 2 cups confectioners' sugar
- 1 teaspoon pure vanilla extract
- 1 to 2 tablespoons milk
- Vanilla wafer cookies and banana slices, for topping

1. Make the cupcakes: Preheat the oven to 350˚. Line a 12-cup muffin pan with cupcake liners. Whisk together the flour, ground cookies, baking powder and salt in a medium bowl.

2. Beat the butter and granulated sugar in a large bowl with a mixer on medium-high speed until light and fluffy, scraping down the bowl occasionally, 3 to 5 minutes. Beat in the eggs, one at a time, until fully combined. Combine the milk and vanilla in a liquid measuring cup. With the mixer on low speed, beat the flour mixture into the butter mixture in 2 batches, alternating with the milk mixture. Add the chopped banana and stir with a rubber spatula until blended.

3. Divide the batter among the muffin cups, filling each about three-quarters of the way. Bake until the cupcakes are golden and spring back when pressed, 25 to 30 minutes. Transfer to a rack and let cool 5 minutes in the pan, then transfer the cupcakes to a rack to cool completely.

4. Meanwhile, make the filling: Put the white chocolate chips in a small heatproof bowl. Heat the heavy cream in the microwave until steaming, then pour over the white chocolate; let stand until softened, 3 to 5 minutes; stir until smooth. Let cool about 15 minutes, then refrigerate until thick, stirring, 5 to 15 minutes. The filling should fall off a spoon in a thick ribbon.

5. Make the frosting: Beat the butter and salt in a large bowl with a mixer on medium-high speed until creamy, 1 to 2 minutes. Beat in the confectioners' sugar on low speed, then increase the speed to medium-high and beat until fluffy, 2 to 3 minutes. Add the vanilla and 1 tablespoon milk and beat until smooth, about 1 more minute. Beat in the remaining 1 tablespoon milk if the frosting is too stiff.

6. Cut a 1-inch-wide slit in the top of each cupcake, slicing about halfway down. Transfer the filling to a piping bag fitted with a small round tip. Gently squeeze each cupcake to open and pipe the filling into the cupcakes. Spread or pipe the frosting on the cupcakes; top each with a cookie and a banana slice.

A mix of spices and grapefruit zest in these cupcakes mimics the strong, slightly bitter flavor of a Negroni. The finishing touch: Campari frosting!

Negroni Cupcakes

ACTIVE: 45 min **I** TOTAL: 1 hr 10 min (plus cooling) **I** MAKES: 12

FOR THE CUPCAKES

- 1½ cups all-purpose flour
- 1 teaspoon baking powder
- ½ teaspoon salt
- 1 teaspoon ground cardamom
- ¾ teaspoon ground pink peppercorns
- ⅛ teaspoon ground black pepper
- 1 stick unsalted butter, at room temperature
- 1 cup granulated sugar
- 2 tablespoons finely grated grapefruit zest
- ½ cup whole milk
- 2 large egg whites

FOR THE FROSTING

- 2 sticks unsalted butter, at room temperature
- 3 cups confectioners' sugar
- 3 tablespoons Campari (or grapefruit juice)

Red and orange gel food coloring

Orange coarse sugar, for decorating

Small orange slices, for decorating

1 Make the cupcakes: Preheat the oven to 350°. Line a 12-cup muffin pan with cupcake liners. Whisk together the flour, baking powder, salt, cardamom and both peppers in a medium bowl.

2 In a large bowl, beat the butter, granulated sugar and grapefruit zest with a mixer on medium-high speed until light and fluffy, about 3 minutes. Reduce the speed to medium-low and beat in the flour mixture in 3 additions, alternating with the milk, beginning and ending with the flour mixture, until just combined.

3 In a clean bowl with clean beaters, beat the egg whites on high speed until they hold stiff peaks but are not dry and clumpy, about 4 minutes. Gently fold the egg whites into the batter until no white streaks remain.

4 Divide the batter among the muffin cups. Bake until the cupcakes are golden and a toothpick inserted into the center of a cupcake comes out clean, 22 to 24 minutes. Let cool 5 minutes in the pan, then transfer the cupcakes to a rack to cool completely.

5 Meanwhile, make the frosting: Beat the butter and confectioners' sugar in a large bowl with a mixer on medium speed until combined, then increase the speed to medium-high and beat until smooth and fluffy, about 3 minutes. Beat in the Campari (or grapefruit juice), then tint with red and orange food coloring until Campari-colored. Spread the frosting on the cupcakes with an offset spatula. Sprinkle with coarse sugar and top each with an orange slice.

This frosting is a custard, so it's much softer than buttercream. If it's too soft to pipe, just refrigerate it until it firms up a bit.

Champagne-Vanilla Cupcakes

ACTIVE: 1 hr I TOTAL: 2 hr (plus cooling) I MAKES: 12

FOR THE CUPCAKES

- 1 half-bottle (375 ml) sparkling white wine (about 1½ cups)
- 1 teaspoon pure vanilla extract
- 1 cup all-purpose flour
- 1½ teaspoons baking powder
- ½ teaspoon kosher salt
- 6 tablespoons unsalted butter, at room temperature
- ¾ cup sugar
- 1 vanilla bean, split lengthwise and seeds scraped (pod reserved for the frosting)
- 1 large egg, separated

FOR THE CUSTARD FROSTING

- 2 teaspoons unflavored gelatin powder
- ½ cup sugar
- ¼ teaspoon kosher salt
- 4 large egg yolks
- ½ cup cold heavy cream

Sugar pearls, for decorating

1 Make the cupcakes: Preheat the oven to 350°. Line a 12-cup muffin pan with cupcake liners. Pour the sparkling wine into a bowl and whisk until the bubbles dissipate. Combine ½ cup of the sparkling wine and the vanilla extract in a small bowl. Reserve the remaining sparkling wine for the frosting.

2 Whisk together the flour, baking powder and salt in a bowl. Beat the butter, sugar and vanilla seeds in a large bowl with a mixer on medium-high speed until light and fluffy, about 5 minutes. Add the egg yolk and beat until smooth. Reduce the mixer speed to low; beat in the flour mixture in 2 batches, alternating with the champagne-vanilla mixture in 2 batches, until just combined. In a separate bowl, whisk the egg white until stiff peaks form, then gently fold the egg white into the batter with a rubber spatula.

3 Divide the batter among the muffin cups, filling each about two-thirds of the way. Bake until the tops of the cupcakes spring back when gently pressed, 20 to 25 minutes. Let cool 5 minutes in the pan, then transfer the cupcakes to a rack to cool completely.

4 Make the frosting: Put 1½ tablespoons of the reserved sparkling wine in a bowl; sprinkle the gelatin on top and let stand. Whisk the sugar, salt and egg yolks in a small saucepan until smooth. Whisk in the remaining sparkling wine; add the reserved vanilla pod. Cook over medium heat, whisking, until the custard is thick enough to coat a spoon, 3 to 4 minutes. Pour the hot custard through a fine-mesh sieve into a metal bowl, discarding the vanilla pod. Stir in the gelatin mixture to dissolve. Refrigerate, stirring, until the consistency of soft whipped cream, 10 to 20 minutes.

5 Beat the heavy cream in a medium bowl with a mixer on medium speed until stiff peaks form. Add the whipped cream to the cooled custard and gently whisk until combined. Refrigerate the frosting, folding with a rubber spatula every 5 minutes, until thick, 10 to 20 minutes.

6 Working quickly, transfer the frosting to a piping bag fitted with a large round tip; pipe onto the cupcakes. Decorate with sugar pearls. Refrigerate to set the frosting, about 30 minutes.

The candied carrots on top of these cupcakes are easy to make: Just use a vegetable peeler to make carrot ribbons, then cook in a simple syrup.

Carrot-Walnut Cupcakes

ACTIVE: 1 hr **|** TOTAL: 1½ hr (plus cooling) **|** MAKES: 12

FOR THE CUPCAKES

- 1   cup all-purpose flour
- ¾   teaspoon baking powder
- ½   teaspoon baking soda
- ¾   teaspoon salt
- 1   teaspoon ground cinnamon
- ¼   teaspoon ground nutmeg
- 2   large eggs
- ½   cup granulated sugar
- ⅓   cup packed light brown sugar
- ⅓   cup unsalted butter, melted
- ⅓   cup walnut oil or vegetable oil
- 1   teaspoon pure vanilla extract
- 1¾ cups finely grated carrots
     (about 2 medium)
- ½   cup walnuts, roughly chopped
- 1   tablespoon finely chopped
     candied ginger

FOR THE CANDIED CARROTS AND WALNUTS

Cooking spray
- 1   large carrot, peeled
- ¾   cup granulated sugar
- ¾   cup water
- 12 walnuts

FOR THE FROSTING

- 6   tablespoons unsalted butter,
     at room temperature
- 1   8-ounce package cream
     cheese, at room temperature
- 1   teaspoon pure vanilla extract
- ⅛   teaspoon salt
- 3½ cups confectioners' sugar,
     sifted

1. Make the cupcakes: Preheat the oven to 350°. Line a 12-cup muffin pan with cupcake liners. Whisk together the flour, baking powder, baking soda, salt, cinnamon and nutmeg in a medium bowl. Whisk together the eggs, granulated sugar, brown sugar, melted butter, walnut oil and vanilla in a separate large bowl until smooth. Whisk in the flour mixture, then fold in the grated carrots, chopped walnuts and candied ginger with a rubber spatula.

2. Divide the batter among the muffin cups, filling each two-thirds of the way. Bake until the tops of the cupcakes spring back when gently pressed, about 20 minutes. Let cool 5 minutes in the pan, then transfer the cupcakes to a rack to cool completely.

3. Meanwhile, make the candied carrots and walnuts: Coat a baking sheet with cooking spray. Peel 12 long ribbons from the carrot with a vegetable peeler. Combine the granulated sugar and water in a small saucepan and bring to a boil. Reduce the heat to a simmer, add the carrot ribbons and cook until translucent, 25 to 30 minutes. Carefully remove with tongs and arrange each ribbon in a small bundle on the baking sheet. Add the walnuts to the saucepan and simmer until glossy, about 5 minutes. Transfer to the baking sheet with a slotted spoon; let the carrots and walnuts cool.

4. Make the frosting: Beat the butter, cream cheese, vanilla and salt in a large bowl with a mixer on medium-high speed until smooth. Beat in the confectioners' sugar on low speed; increase the speed to medium-high and beat until fluffy, 3 minutes. Transfer to a piping bag fitted with a large round tip; pipe onto the cupcakes. Top with the candied carrots and walnuts.

Rosewater gives these cupcakes a slightly floral flavor. Don't go overboard; it's very strong!

Raspberry-Rose Cupcakes

ACTIVE: 1 hr 15 min I TOTAL: 2 hr (plus cooling) I MAKES: 12

FOR THE CUPCAKES

1⅓ cups all-purpose flour
½ teaspoon baking powder
½ teaspoon baking soda
½ teaspoon salt
1 stick unsalted butter, melted
¾ cup granulated sugar
½ cup sour cream
2 large eggs
1 teaspoon pure vanilla extract

FOR THE FILLING

2 cups raspberries
1 cup plus 1 tablespoon water
⅔ cup granulated sugar
1½ teaspoons cornstarch
½ teaspoon rosewater

FOR THE FROSTING

1 cup granulated sugar
3 large egg whites
2 sticks unsalted butter,
   cut into pieces,
   at room temperature
¾ to 1 teaspoon rosewater
Coarse sugar, for decorating

1. Make the cupcakes: Preheat the oven to 350°. Line a 12-cup muffin pan with cupcake liners. Whisk the flour, baking powder, baking soda and salt in a bowl. Whisk together the melted butter, granulated sugar, sour cream, eggs and vanilla in a large bowl until smooth. Whisk in the flour mixture until smooth.

2. Divide the batter among the muffin cups, filling each about two-thirds of the way. Bake until the tops of the cupcakes are golden and spring back when pressed, 18 to 20 minutes. Let cool 5 minutes in the pan, then transfer the cupcakes to a rack to cool completely.

3. Meanwhile, make the filling: Combine the raspberries, 1 cup water and the granulated sugar in a medium saucepan; bring to a boil, stirring. Reduce the heat to a simmer and cook until reduced by half, 15 minutes. Whisk together the cornstarch, rosewater and remaining 1 tablespoon water in a bowl. Add to the raspberries and continue to cook, stirring, until thickened, 2 to 3 minutes. Strain the filling through a fine-mesh sieve, pressing on the solids with a spatula. Let cool 20 minutes.

4. Make the frosting: Put the granulated sugar and egg whites in the bowl of a stand mixer; set the bowl over a saucepan of simmering water (do not let the bowl touch the water). Whisk until the sugar dissolves, 3 to 5 minutes. Transfer the bowl to the stand mixer; beat with the whisk attachment on medium-high speed until stiff glossy peaks form, 6 to 8 minutes. Switch to the paddle attachment and beat in the butter a few pieces at a time on medium-high speed. (It's OK if the frosting looks curdled—it will smooth out as you beat.) Once all the butter is added, beat until the frosting is smooth, 1 to 2 minutes. Add the rosewater and 3 to 4 tablespoons of the raspberry filling; beat until smooth.

5. With a paring knife, cut a ¾-inch-deep slit across the top of each cupcake, nearly edge to edge; gently squeeze the sides of the cupcake so the slit opens. Spoon about 1 teaspoon of the raspberry filling into each cupcake. Let stand 5 minutes, then spoon the remaining filling into the cupcakes. Spread the frosting on the cupcakes. Sprinkle with coarse sugar.

If you don't have buttermilk, add a dash of lemon juice or vinegar to regular milk and let it sit 5 minutes before using.

Peaches-and-Cream Cupcakes

ACTIVE: 1 hr 20 min **I** TOTAL: 2 hr (plus cooling) **I** MAKES: 12

FOR THE CUPCAKES

1½ cups all-purpose flour

1½ teaspoons baking powder

½ teaspoon baking soda

¼ teaspoon salt

1 stick unsalted butter, at room temperature

¾ cup granulated sugar

2 large eggs

1 teaspoon pure vanilla extract

⅛ to ¼ teaspoon pure almond extract

⅔ cup buttermilk

FOR THE PEACHES

2 tablespoons unsalted butter

2 small ripe peaches, each cut into 6 wedges

1 tablespoon granulated sugar

FOR THE FROSTING

2 sticks unsalted butter, at room temperature

2½ cups confectioners' sugar

3 tablespoons whole milk

¼ teaspoon pure vanilla extract

¼ teaspoon pure almond extract

1 Make the cupcakes: Preheat the oven to 350°. Line a 12-cup muffin pan with cupcake liners. Whisk together the flour, baking powder, baking soda and salt in a medium bowl. Beat the butter and granulated sugar in a large bowl with a mixer on medium-high speed until light and fluffy, about 3 minutes. Beat in the eggs one at a time, then beat in the vanilla and almond extracts. Reduce the mixer speed to low and beat in half of the flour mixture, then the buttermilk, then the remaining flour mixture until smooth.

2 Divide the batter among the muffin cups, filling each about two-thirds of the way. Bake until the tops of the cupcakes are lightly browned and spring back when gently pressed, about 25 minutes. Let cool 5 minutes in the pan, then transfer the cupcakes to a rack to cool completely.

3 Meanwhile, cook the peaches: Melt the butter in a large nonstick skillet over medium heat. Add the peaches and granulated sugar and cook, stirring occasionally, until the sugar dissolves and the peaches start softening, 2 to 3 minutes. Cover and continue to cook, stirring occasionally, until the peaches are soft but still hold their shape, about 5 more minutes. Remove from the heat and let cool completely.

4 Make the frosting: Beat the butter and confectioners' sugar in a large bowl with a mixer on medium speed until smooth. Increase the speed to medium-high and beat until fluffy, 2 to 3 more minutes. Add the milk and vanilla and almond extracts and beat until smooth. Transfer to a piping bag fitted with a large round tip; pipe onto the cupcakes. Refrigerate until the frosting is firm, 20 to 30 minutes. Top each cupcake with a peach wedge.

These cupcakes have a surprise inside: homemade pineapple curd!

100

Piña Colada Cupcakes

ACTIVE: 45 min | TOTAL: 1½ hr (plus cooling) | MAKES: 12

FOR THE PINEAPPLE CURD

- ½ cup granulated sugar
- ½ cup pineapple juice
- ¼ teaspoon kosher salt
- 2 large eggs plus 2 egg yolks
- 2 tablespoons unsalted butter
- 1 tablespoon white rum (optional)

FOR THE CUPCAKES

- 1½ cups all-purpose flour
- 1 teaspoon baking powder
- ½ teaspoon kosher salt
- 1 stick unsalted butter, at room temperature
- ¾ cup granulated sugar
- ¼ cup packed light brown sugar
- 2 large eggs
- 1 teaspoon pure vanilla extract
- ½ cup whole milk

FOR THE FROSTING

- 1½ sticks (12 tablespoons) unsalted butter, at room temperature
- 3 cups confectioners' sugar
- ½ teaspoon coconut extract
- 3 tablespoons whole milk
- 1½ cups sweetened shredded coconut

1. Make the pineapple curd: Whisk together the granulated sugar, pineapple juice and salt in a medium saucepan. Whisk in the eggs and egg yolks until combined. Cook over medium heat, whisking constantly and reducing the heat if the mixture starts bubbling too much, until the curd is the consistency of pudding, 7 to 8 minutes (you should have a little over 1 cup).

2. Remove the curd from the heat and whisk in the butter and rum (if using). Strain the curd through a fine-mesh sieve into a bowl, pressing it through with a rubber spatula. Cover with plastic wrap, pressing it directly onto the surface, and refrigerate until completely cooled, about 2 hours.

3. Meanwhile, make the cupcakes: Preheat the oven to 350°. Line a 12-cup muffin pan with cupcake liners. Whisk together the flour, baking powder and salt in a medium bowl. Combine the butter, granulated sugar and brown sugar in another large bowl; beat with a mixer on medium-high speed until light and fluffy, 3 to 4 minutes. Beat in the eggs, one at a time, then beat in the vanilla. With the mixer on medium speed, beat in the flour mixture in 2 batches, alternating with the milk, until combined.

4. Divide the batter among the muffin cups, filling them about two-thirds of the way. Bake until a toothpick inserted into the center of a cupcake comes out clean, 20 to 25 minutes. Let cool 10 minutes in the pan, then transfer the cupcakes to a rack to cool completely.

5. Make the frosting: Combine the butter and confectioners' sugar in a large bowl; beat with a mixer on medium-high speed until smooth and fluffy, 2 to 3 minutes. Add the coconut extract and milk and beat until smooth.

6. Using a paring knife, cut a slit in the top of each cupcake, cutting about three-quarters of the way down. Fill a piping bag with the pineapple curd; pipe the curd into the slit in each cupcake. Fill another piping bag with the frosting and pipe onto the cupcakes (or spread the frosting on the cupcakes). Top with the shredded coconut.

This is a meringue frosting, so it tastes like marshmallow, especially when you toast it!

Pumpkin Cupcakes with Toasted Marshmallow Frosting

ACTIVE: 1 hr | TOTAL: 1½ hr (plus cooling) | MAKES: 24

FOR THE CUPCAKES

2½ cups all-purpose flour

2 teaspoons ground cinnamon

1 teaspoon baking powder

1 teaspoon baking soda

1 teaspoon kosher salt

½ teaspoon ground nutmeg

½ teaspoon ground cloves

2 cups packed light brown sugar

4 large eggs

2 sticks unsalted butter, melted

1 15-ounce can pure pumpkin puree

2 teaspoons pure vanilla extract

FOR THE FROSTING

⅔ cup granulated sugar

¼ teaspoon cream of tartar

4 large egg whites

Pinch of salt

2 teaspoons pure vanilla extract

1. Make the cupcakes: Position racks in the upper and lower thirds of the oven and preheat to 350°. Line two 12-cup muffin pans with cupcake liners. Whisk together the flour, cinnamon, baking powder, baking soda, salt, nutmeg and cloves in a medium bowl. Combine the brown sugar, eggs, melted butter, pumpkin puree and vanilla in a large bowl and whisk until smooth. Add the flour mixture and whisk until just combined.

2. Divide the batter among the muffin cups, filling each about two-thirds of the way. Bake, switching the pans halfway through, until the tops of the cupcakes spring back when gently pressed, 25 to 30 minutes. Let cool 5 minutes in the pans, then transfer the cupcakes to racks to cool completely.

3. Meanwhile, make the frosting: Combine the granulated sugar, cream of tartar, egg whites and salt in a large heatproof bowl set over a saucepan of simmering water (do not let the bowl touch the water). Whisk until the mixture is warm and the sugar dissolves, 2 to 3 minutes. Remove the bowl from the pan, add the vanilla and beat with a mixer on medium-high speed until the frosting is cool and stiff glossy peaks form, 4 to 6 minutes.

4. Transfer the frosting to a piping bag fitted with a large round tip; pipe onto the cupcakes. Brown the frosting with a kitchen torch.

You can fill these cupcakes with anything you like. Try Nutella, dulce de leche or lemon curd!

Jelly Doughnut Cupcakes

ACTIVE: 1 hr **I** TOTAL: 1½ hr (plus cooling) **I** MAKES: 12

FOR THE CUPCAKES

1⅓ cups all-purpose flour

1 teaspoon baking powder

½ teaspoon salt

1 stick unsalted butter, at room temperature

1 cup granulated sugar

2 large eggs

2 teaspoons pure vanilla extract

½ cup milk

½ cup seedless raspberry or strawberry jam

FOR THE FROSTING

1½ sticks (12 tablespoons) unsalted butter, at room temperature

3 cups confectioners' sugar

Pinch of salt

2 teaspoons pure vanilla extract

2 tablespoons milk

Coarse sugar, for topping

1. Make the cupcakes: Preheat the oven to 350°. Line a 12-cup muffin pan with cupcake liners. Whisk the flour, baking powder and salt in a medium bowl.

2. Beat the butter in a large bowl with a mixer on medium-high speed until smooth, 1 minute. Add the granulated sugar and beat until creamy, about 4 minutes. Beat in the eggs, one at a time, then the vanilla. Beat in the flour mixture in 3 batches on low speed, alternating with the milk. Beat on medium-high speed until just combined.

3. Divide the batter among the muffin cups, filling each about two-thirds of the way. Bake until the tops of the cupcakes spring back when pressed, 20 to 25 minutes. Let cool 5 minutes in the pan, then transfer the cupcakes to a rack to cool completely.

4. Fit a piping bag with a large open tip; fill with the jam. With a paring knife, cut a 1-inch-wide slit in the top of each cupcake, slicing about halfway down. Insert the piping bag into the slit and pipe in the jam.

5. Make the frosting: Beat the butter, confectioners' sugar and salt in a large bowl with a mixer on medium speed until just combined. Add the vanilla and beat on medium-high speed until creamy, about 3 minutes. Beat in the milk until fluffy, about 1 minute. Spread or pipe the frosting on the cupcakes. Sprinkle with coarse sugar.

Brown butter gives these cupcakes extra caramel-like flavor. Keep an eye on the butter as it cooks; it will darken quickly.

Caramel Corn Cupcakes

ACTIVE: 45 min | TOTAL: 1 hr 15 min (plus cooling) | MAKES: 12

FOR THE CUPCAKES

1   stick unsalted butter
1   cup granulated sugar
2   large eggs
½   cup whole milk
1   teaspoon pure vanilla extract
1   cup all-purpose flour
⅓   cup almond flour
1   teaspoon baking powder
½   teaspoon salt

FOR THE FROSTING

1½ sticks (12 tablespoons) unsalted butter, at room temperature
2   cups confectioners' sugar
¾   teaspoon pumpkin pie spice
⅛   teaspoon salt
½   teaspoon pure vanilla extract
½   cup dulce de leche
Caramel corn, for topping

1. Make the cupcakes: Preheat the oven to 350°. Line a 12-cup muffin pan with cupcake liners. Melt the butter in a small skillet over medium heat; cook, swirling the pan occasionally, until the butter is browned, 6 to 9 minutes. Immediately transfer to a medium bowl and let cool slightly. Whisk in the granulated sugar, eggs, milk and vanilla.

2. Whisk the all-purpose flour, almond flour, baking powder and salt in a large bowl. Add the brown butter mixture and whisk until just combined (do not overmix).

3. Divide the batter among the muffin cups, filling them three-quarters of the way. Bake until the tops of the cupcakes spring back when gently pressed, 18 to 22 minutes. Let cool 5 minutes in the pan, then transfer the cupcakes to a rack to cool completely.

4. Make the frosting: Beat the butter, confectioners' sugar, pumpkin pie spice and salt in a large bowl with a mixer on medium speed until just combined. Increase the mixer speed to medium-high, add the vanilla and beat until fluffy, about 3 minutes. Swirl in the dulce de leche with a rubber spatula, leaving some streaks. Transfer to a piping bag fitted with a round tip. Pipe onto the cupcakes and top with caramel corn.

Cakes

Red Velvet–Cream Cheese Bundt Cake

ACTIVE: 45 min I TOTAL: 2 hr (plus cooling) I SERVES: 8 to 10

FOR THE SWIRL

2   8-ounce packages cream cheese
⅔   cup granulated sugar
2   large eggs
3   tablespoons sour cream
3   tablespoons heavy cream
1   teaspoon pure vanilla extract

FOR THE CAKE

Cooking spray
2½ cups all-purpose flour, plus more for the pan
1¾ cups granulated sugar
2   tablespoons unsweetened cocoa powder
1   teaspoon baking soda
1   teaspoon salt
1½ cups vegetable oil
¾   cup sour cream
2   large eggs, at room temperature
1½ teaspoons red gel food coloring
1   teaspoon pure vanilla extract
1   teaspoon distilled white vinegar
¼   cup water

FOR THE GLAZE

4   ounces cream cheese
½   cup confectioners' sugar
½   cup sour cream
1   teaspoon pure vanilla extract
Pinch of salt

1 Make the swirl: Combine the cream cheese, granulated sugar, eggs, sour cream, heavy cream and vanilla in a food processor. Puree until smooth.

2 Make the cake: Position a rack in the lower third of the oven and preheat to 350°. Generously coat a 10- to 15-cup bundt pan with cooking spray and dust with flour, tapping out the excess. Whisk the flour, granulated sugar, cocoa powder, baking soda and salt in a large bowl. Whisk the vegetable oil, sour cream, eggs, food coloring, vanilla, vinegar and water in a medium bowl. Pour the sour cream mixture into the flour mixture and whisk to combine.

3 Spread 3 cups of the cake batter in the prepared pan. Pour in the cream cheese swirl mixture, then spoon the remaining cake batter evenly over the top. Bake until the top is cracked and a toothpick inserted into the cake comes out clean, about 1 hour 10 minutes. Transfer to a rack and let cool 20 minutes in the pan, then carefully invert onto a plate to cool completely, at least 2 hours.

4 Make the glaze: Combine the cream cheese, confectioners' sugar, sour cream, vanilla and salt in a food processor and puree until smooth. Pour the glaze on the cooled cake and spread with an offset spatula.

Bundt pans have lots of ridges, so you need to grease the pan well. Coat it generously with cooking spray, then dust very lightly with flour.

Nectarine Upside-Down Cake with Salted Caramel

ACTIVE: 30 min **|** TOTAL: 1 hr 20 min (plus cooling) **|** SERVES: 6 to 8

Cooking spray

1¾ cups sugar

1   teaspoon fine salt

1½ tablespoons water

4   nectarines, cut into ½-inch
    wedges (about 1¼ pounds)

1¾ cups all-purpose flour

1   teaspoon baking powder

½   teaspoon baking soda

1   stick unsalted butter,
    at room temperature

2   large eggs

1   teaspoon pure vanilla
    extract

1   cup buttermilk

Flaky salt, for sprinkling

1 Preheat the oven to 375°. Coat a 9-inch square cake pan with cooking spray. Combine ¾ cup sugar, ½ teaspoon fine salt and the water in a medium saucepan and stir until the mixture looks like wet sand. Cook over medium-high heat, gently swirling the pan occasionally but not stirring, until light amber, about 5 minutes. Remove from the heat and immediately pour into the prepared cake pan (the caramel hardens quickly). Arrange the nectarines over the caramel in 4 rows.

2 Whisk together the flour, baking powder, baking soda and remaining ½ teaspoon fine salt in a medium bowl. Beat the butter and remaining 1 cup sugar in a large bowl with a mixer on medium-high speed until light and fluffy, about 3 minutes Add the eggs one at a time, beating until combined after each addition, then beat in the vanilla. Reduce the mixer speed to low and add the flour mixture in 3 batches, alternating with the buttermilk, beginning and ending with the flour; mix until just combined. Pour the batter over the nectarines and spread evenly.

3 Bake until the cake is golden and a toothpick inserted into the center comes out clean, about 50 minutes; cover loosely with foil if the cake is browning too quickly. Let cool 15 minutes in the pan, then invert onto a platter to cool completely. Sprinkle with flaky salt.

Flaky salt is a great finishing salt for desserts; it adds flavor and crunch. Avoid flaky salt for batters though, as the crystals are irregular in shape and won't disperse evenly.

Angel food cake
should be baked in
an ungreased pan
so the batter can cling
to the sides of the
pan as it rises.

Rosemary Angel Food Cake with Pineapple Compote

ACTIVE: 50 min **I** TOTAL: 1 hr 20 min (plus cooling) **I** SERVES: 8 to 10

FOR THE CAKE

1 cup cake flour

1¾ cups superfine sugar

½ teaspoon salt

12 large egg whites, at room temperature

1½ teaspoons cream of tartar

1½ teaspoons pure vanilla extract

2 teaspoons finely chopped fresh rosemary

2 teaspoons finely chopped fresh thyme

Finely grated zest of 2 lemons

FOR THE COMPOTE

½ cup packed light brown sugar

½ cup dark rum

½ cup water

1 sprig rosemary

1 sprig thyme

1 medium pineapple, peeled, cored and cut into ½-inch pieces

2 teaspoons pure vanilla extract

1 Make the cake: Preheat the oven to 350°. Sift the cake flour, ¾ cup superfine sugar and the salt onto a piece of parchment paper. Sift the flour mixture a second time onto another piece of parchment.

2 Beat the egg whites in a large bowl with a mixer on medium-high speed until frothy, about 1 minute. Add the cream of tartar and continue beating until soft peaks form, about 4 minutes. Gradually beat in the remaining 1 cup superfine sugar; increase the speed to high and beat until the egg whites are stiff and glossy, about 7 minutes. Beat in the vanilla, rosemary, thyme and lemon zest.

3 Using a rubber spatula, fold the flour mixture into the egg white mixture, ¼ cup at a time, until fully combined with no pockets of dry ingredients. Transfer the batter to an ungreased 10-inch angel food cake pan. Bake until golden and the cake springs back when pressed, 40 to 45 minutes. Invert the cake pan onto a small funnel or bottle neck and let cool completely, at least 1 hour.

4 Meanwhile, make the compote: Combine the brown sugar, rum, water and rosemary and thyme sprigs in a medium saucepan over medium-high heat. Simmer, stirring, until the sugar dissolves, about 2 minutes. Add the pineapple, return to a gentle simmer and cook until the pineapple is softened and the liquid is syrupy, about 10 minutes. Stir in the vanilla. Transfer to a bowl and refrigerate, stirring occasionally, until cool, about 1 hour. Discard the herb sprigs.

5 Loosen the edge of the cake with a knife, tap the sides of the pan against the counter and unmold the cake onto a platter. Slice with a long serrated knife and serve with the compote.

You'll need to work quickly when the cake comes out of the oven. Invert it onto a towel and roll it up while it's still warm; if it cools before you roll it, it may crack.

Lemon-Vanilla Cake Roll

ACTIVE: 1½ hr I TOTAL: 1 hr 45 min (plus cooling) I SERVES: 8 to 10

FOR THE CAKE

Cooking spray

6   large eggs, separated, at room temperature

½   teaspoon fresh lemon juice

1½ cups confectioners' sugar, plus more for dusting

¼   cup vegetable oil

¼   cup whole milk

1   vanilla bean, split lengthwise and seeds scraped

1¼ cups all-purpose flour

½   teaspoon baking powder

¼   teaspoon salt

FOR THE FROSTING AND FILLING

5   large egg whites

1⅓ cups granulated sugar

1   vanilla bean, split lengthwise and seeds scraped

Pinch of salt

3   sticks unsalted butter, cut into pieces, at room temperature

1   tablespoon finely grated lemon zest, plus 2 tablespoons fresh lemon juice

½   cup lemon curd

1 Make the cake: Preheat the oven to 375°. Coat an 11-by-17-inch rimmed baking sheet with cooking spray; line the bottom with parchment paper and spray the parchment. Beat the egg whites and lemon juice in a large bowl with a mixer on medium speed until soft peaks form, 3 minutes. Add ½ cup confectioners' sugar. Beat on medium speed until stiff peaks form, 3 to 4 minutes.

2 Whisk together the egg yolks, vegetable oil, milk and vanilla seeds in another large bowl until smooth. Sift the remaining 1 cup confectioners' sugar, the flour, baking powder and salt into a separate bowl; whisk into the yolk mixture until smooth. Stir about one-third of the beaten egg whites into the batter with a rubber spatula, then fold in the remaining egg whites in 2 batches. Spread the batter in the prepared pan. Bake until the cake springs back when gently pressed, 12 to 14 minutes.

3 Sift confectioners' sugar generously over the top of the warm cake and loosen the edges with a knife; lay a clean kitchen towel (not terry cloth) over the cake. Place another baking sheet over the towel and flip the cake between the pans to invert it onto the towel. Remove the top baking sheet and discard the parchment. Starting at a short end, roll up the cake and towel together into a spiral. Place seam-side down on a rack to cool completely.

4 Meanwhile, make the frosting: Whisk together the egg whites, granulated sugar, vanilla seeds and salt in a heatproof bowl set over a saucepan of simmering water (do not let the bowl touch the water). Cook, whisking, until the sugar dissolves, 2 to 3 minutes. Transfer the mixture to a stand mixer and beat with the whisk attachment on medium-high speed until stiff peaks form, 6 to 8 minutes. Beat in the butter, 1 piece at a time (the mixture may look curdled at first; just keep beating). Add the lemon zest and juice. Switch to the paddle attachment and beat until smooth, about 2 minutes.

5 Gently unroll the cake. Spread 2 cups of the frosting on the cake, leaving a ¼-inch border. Top with the lemon curd and swirl with an offset spatula. Reroll the cake. Transfer to a platter and cover with the remaining frosting.

To get a super-flat surface on your layer cakes, trim the domed tops of the cakes to make them level. Then stack the cakes with frosting in between, arranging the top layer trimmed-side down.

Double Chocolate Cake

ACTIVE: 45 min I TOTAL: 2 hr (plus cooling) I SERVES: 8 to 10

FOR THE CAKE

- 1½ sticks (12 tablespoons) unsalted butter, at room temperature, plus more for the pans
- 2 cups all-purpose flour, plus more for the pans
- ⅔ cup unsweetened cocoa powder (not dutch-process)
- 2 ounces semisweet chocolate, chopped
- 1 cup boiling water
- ½ cup sour cream
- 1¼ teaspoons baking soda
- ½ teaspoon salt
- 1 cup granulated sugar
- ¾ cup packed dark brown sugar
- 4 large eggs, at room temperature
- 2 teaspoons pure vanilla extract

FOR THE FROSTING

- 6 large egg whites, at room temperature
- 1 cup granulated sugar
- ¼ teaspoon salt
- 4 sticks unsalted butter, cut into small pieces, at room temperature
- 1 teaspoon pure vanilla extract
- 8 ounces semisweet chocolate, chopped

1 Make the cake: Preheat the oven to 350°. Butter the bottom and sides of two 9-inch round cake pans; flour the pans. Put the cocoa powder and chocolate in a bowl. Pour in the boiling water; whisk until smooth. Whisk in the sour cream. Let cool.

2 Whisk together the flour, baking soda and salt in a medium bowl. Beat the butter and both sugars in a large bowl with a mixer on medium-high speed until fluffy, 3 to 4 minutes. Beat in the eggs one at a time, then the vanilla. Reduce the mixer speed to low; beat in the flour mixture in 3 batches, alternating with the cocoa mixture. Divide the batter between the pans.

3 Bake the cakes until a toothpick inserted into the centers comes out clean, 35 to 40 minutes. Transfer to a rack and let cool 15 minutes in the pans, then turn out the cakes onto the rack to cool completely; discard the parchment.

4 Meanwhile, make the frosting: Bring a few inches of water to a simmer in a saucepan over medium heat. Whisk together the egg whites, sugar and salt in the bowl of a stand mixer. Set the bowl on top of the pan of water (do not let the bowl touch the water). Cook, whisking, until the egg whites are frothy, the sugar dissolves and the mixture is warm, 3 to 5 minutes.

5 Transfer the bowl to the mixer and beat the mixture with the whisk attachment on medium-high speed until stiff glossy peaks form, 5 minutes. Beat in the butter a few pieces at a time (the mixture may look curdled at first; just keep beating). Add the vanilla and beat until fluffy, 3 to 5 more minutes. Melt the chocolate in the microwave, then let cool slightly. Using the paddle attachment, beat the melted chocolate into the frosting.

6 Trim the domed tops of the cake layers, if desired. Place one layer on a cake stand and spread with 1 cup frosting. Top with the second layer, trimmed-side down. Spread a thin layer of frosting over the top and sides of the cake (this is the crumb coat; it doesn't have to be perfect). Refrigerate 30 minutes.

7 Cover the cake with more frosting, then run an offset spatula around the side of the cake to create a ridge in the frosting. Work your way up the cake to make more ridges.

Cake flour has a
low protein content,
so it's good for tender
cakes like this one.
If you don't have any,
use all-purpose flour
but for every cup of flour,
replace 2 tablespoons
with cornstarch.

Coconut Layer Cake

ACTIVE: 40 min I TOTAL: 2 hr (plus cooling) I SERVES: 10 to 12

FOR THE CAKE

- 2 sticks unsalted butter, at room temperature, plus more for the pans
- 2¾ cups cake flour, plus more for the pans
- 1½ teaspoons baking powder
- ½ teaspoon baking soda
- ½ teaspoon salt
- ¾ cup buttermilk
- ½ cup sweetened cream of coconut (from one 15-ounce can), stirred well
- 1¾ cups granulated sugar
- 4 large eggs, at room temperature, separated
- 2 teaspoons pure vanilla extract
- 1 teaspoon coconut extract

FOR THE FROSTING

- 2 sticks unsalted butter, at room temperature
- 12 ounces cream cheese, at room temperature
- 3½ cups confectioners' sugar
- ½ teaspoon salt
- 1 teaspoon pure vanilla extract
- 1 teaspoon coconut extract
- 2 cups sweetened shredded coconut

1 Make the cake: Position racks in the middle and lower third of the oven; preheat to 350°. Butter three 9-inch round cake pans and line the bottoms with parchment paper; butter the parchment, dust with flour and tap out the excess.

2 Whisk together the flour, baking powder, baking soda and salt in a bowl. Whisk together the buttermilk and cream of coconut in a small bowl. Beat the butter and 1¼ cups granulated sugar in a large bowl with a mixer on medium-high speed until light and fluffy, about 4 minutes. Add the egg yolks, one at a time, beating well after each addition, then beat in the vanilla and coconut extracts. Reduce the mixer speed to low; beat in the flour mixture in 3 batches, alternating with the buttermilk mixture, until combined.

3 Beat the egg whites and remaining ½ cup granulated sugar in another large bowl with clean beaters on medium-high speed until stiff glossy peaks form, 4 to 5 minutes. Using a rubber spatula, fold the egg whites into the batter in 3 batches until combined (do not overmix). Divide the batter among the pans and bake, switching the pans halfway through, until the cakes are lightly browned and the centers spring back when lightly pressed, 30 to 35 minutes. Transfer to racks and let cool 20 minutes in the pans, then carefully invert the cakes onto the racks to cool completely; discard the parchment.

4 Meanwhile, make the frosting: Beat the butter and cream cheese in a large bowl with a mixer on medium-high speed until smooth, about 2 minutes. Reduce the mixer speed to low and beat in about half of the confectioners' sugar until combined. Add the remaining confectioners' sugar, salt and vanilla and coconut extracts; beat until combined. Increase the mixer speed to medium-high and beat, scraping down the bowl as needed, until light and fluffy, about 3 minutes.

5 Place one cake layer on a cake stand and top with a heaping ⅔ cup frosting. Add another cake layer, more frosting and the last cake layer. Cover the top and sides of the cake with the remaining frosting. Sprinkle the coconut all over the top and sides of the cake, gently pressing to adhere.

Ricotta cheesecake has a different texture than the cream cheese kind: It's generally lighter, less dense and a little grainy (in a good way!).

Pistachio-Ricotta Cheesecake

ACTIVE: 45 min **I** TOTAL: 3 hr (plus cooling and chilling) **I** SERVES: 10 to 12

FOR THE CRUST

⅓ cup roasted unsalted pistachios, plus 2 tablespoons chopped for topping

5 ounces shortbread cookies (about 16 cookies), such as Lorna Doone

2 tablespoons granulated sugar

3 tablespoons unsalted butter, melted

FOR THE FILLING

3 large eggs

¾ cup granulated sugar

1 pound fresh ricotta cheese (about 2 packed cups)

½ cup unsweetened pistachio paste, stirred if separated

½ teaspoon grated lemon zest

½ teaspoon pure vanilla extract

¼ teaspoon almond extract

¼ teaspoon salt

4 drops green gel food coloring

Confectioners' sugar, for dusting

1 Make the crust: Position a rack in the lower third of the oven and preheat to 325°. Spread the whole and chopped pistachios on a rimmed baking sheet (keep them separated) and bake until toasted, about 10 minutes. Let cool.

2 Set aside the chopped pistachios in a small bowl. Pulse the toasted whole pistachios in a food processor along with the shortbread cookies and granulated sugar until finely ground. Add the melted butter and pulse until the mixture looks like wet sand. Press the mixture into the bottom of an 8-inch round springform pan. Bake until set around the edges and no longer puffed, about 20 minutes. Transfer to a rack; let cool 10 minutes.

3 Meanwhile, make the filling: Beat the eggs and granulated sugar in a large bowl with a mixer on medium-high speed until pale and thickened, about 5 minutes. Add the ricotta, pistachio paste, lemon zest, the vanilla and almond extracts and salt and continue beating until smooth, about 2 minutes. Add the green food coloring and beat until combined.

4 Pour the filling over the crust. Bake until the cheesecake is puffed and the edges are set but the center still jiggles slightly, about 1½ hours.

5 Transfer the cheesecake to a rack and let cool to room temperature, 2 to 3 hours. Run a thin knife around the edges of the cheesecake to loosen, then remove the springform ring. Serve at room temperature or cover and refrigerate until chilled, at least 2 hours or overnight. Dust with confectioners' sugar and sprinkle with the reserved toasted pistachios before serving.

For a thinner sheet cake, use a 13-by-18-inch sheet pan and bake the cake 30 to 35 minutes.

Chocolate-Cherry Sheet Cake

ACTIVE: 45 min I TOTAL: 1 hr 45 min (plus cooling) I SERVES: 8 to 10

FOR THE CAKE

Unsalted butter, for the pan

¾ cup dutch-process cocoa powder, plus more for the pans

2¼ cups all-purpose flour

1¼ teaspoons baking soda

¾ teaspoon salt

½ teaspoon baking powder

1 cup boiling water

2 cups granulated sugar

½ cup vegetable oil

½ cup buttermilk

2 large eggs, at room temperature

1 teaspoon almond extract

1 teaspoon cherry extract

¼ cup cherry preserves

1 tablespoon maraschino liqueur or juice

FOR THE FROSTING

3 sticks unsalted butter, at room temperature

Pinch of salt

4 cups confectioners' sugar

1 tablespoon pure vanilla extract

1 teaspoon cherry extract

3 tablespoons whole milk

Maraschino cherries, for topping

Shaved chocolate, for topping

1 Make the cake: Preheat the oven to 350°. Butter a 9-by-13-inch baking pan. Dust the bottom and sides of the pan with cocoa powder.

2 Whisk together the flour, baking soda, salt and baking powder in a medium bowl. Pour the boiling water over the cocoa powder in a separate bowl; whisk until smooth. Let cool 10 minutes, then whisk in the granulated sugar, vegetable oil, buttermilk, eggs and almond and cherry extracts. Whisk in the flour mixture in 2 batches until smooth.

3 Spread the batter in the baking pan and tap on the counter to release any air bubbles. Bake until a toothpick inserted into the center comes out clean, 35 to 45 minutes. While the cake bakes, combine the cherry preserves and maraschino liqueur or juice in a small bowl. Brush over the warm cake. Transfer the pan to a rack to cool completely before frosting.

4 Make the frosting: Beat the butter and salt with a mixer on medium-high speed until fluffy, about 2 minutes. Gradually beat in the confectioners' sugar on low speed until combined. Add the vanilla and cherry extracts and beat on medium-high speed until fluffy, about 3 minutes. Beat in the milk until combined, 1 to 2 more minutes.

5 Spread the frosting over the cake; top with maraschino cherries and shaved chocolate. Refrigerate 30 minutes before serving.

These cake layers are brushed with coffee liqueur before they're stacked and frosted. This adds tiramisu-like flavor and also keeps the cakes moist.

Tiramisu Layer Cake

ACTIVE: 1½ hr I TOTAL: 2 hr 15 min (plus cooling) I SERVES: 10 to 12

FOR THE CAKE

2 sticks unsalted butter, at room temperature, plus more for the pans

2¼ cups cake flour, plus more for the pans

2 teaspoons baking powder

½ teaspoon salt

1½ cups granulated sugar

4 large eggs

1½ teaspoons pure vanilla extract

¾ cup whole milk

Coffee liqueur, for brushing

FOR THE FILLING

4 ounces cream cheese, at room temperature

½ teaspoon coffee extract

1½ cups plus 1 tablespoon cold heavy cream

½ cup confectioners' sugar

2 teaspoons espresso powder

2 teaspoons unsweetened cocoa powder

FOR THE FROSTING/GANACHE

2½ sticks unsalted butter, at room temperature

8 ounces cream cheese, at room temperature

3½ cups confectioners' sugar

1½ teaspoons coffee extract

1 teaspoon pure vanilla extract

¼ teaspoon salt

½ cup heavy cream

4 ounces semisweet chocolate, finely chopped

1 Make the cake: Preheat the oven to 325°. Butter the bottoms and sides of two 9-inch round cake pans; line the bottoms with parchment paper. Butter the parchment; dust the pans with flour. Whisk together the cake flour, baking powder and salt in a bowl.

2 Beat the butter in a large bowl with a mixer on medium-high speed until creamy, 1 minute. Beat in the granulated sugar until fluffy, 4 minutes. Beat in the eggs one at a time, then the vanilla. Beat in the flour mixture on low speed in 3 batches, alternating with the milk. Beat on medium-high until smooth, 30 seconds.

3 Divide the batter between the cake pans and tap each against the counter. Bake until a toothpick inserted into the centers comes out clean, 30 to 35 minutes. Let cool 15 minutes in the pans, then turn out onto a rack to cool completely; discard the parchment.

4 Meanwhile, make the filling: Beat the cream cheese and coffee extract with a mixer on medium-high speed, 1 minute. If using a stand mixer, switch to the whisk attachment. Beat in 1½ cups heavy cream and the confectioners' sugar until stiff peaks form, 2 minutes. Divide the filling between 2 small bowls. Stir the remaining 1 tablespoon heavy cream with the espresso powder; fold into one of the bowls of filling. Fold the cocoa powder into the other bowl. Refrigerate until ready to use.

5 Make the frosting: Beat the butter and cream cheese in a bowl with a mixer on medium-high speed until smooth, 2 minutes. Reduce the mixer speed to low and beat in the confectioners' sugar, 1 teaspoon coffee extract, the vanilla and salt. Increase the mixer speed to medium-high; beat until fluffy, 4 minutes.

6 Make the ganache: Heat the heavy cream in a saucepan until steaming. Pour over the chopped chocolate in a small bowl; let sit 5 minutes. Stir in the remaining ½ teaspoon coffee extract until smooth; let sit until cool but still pourable, about 1 hour.

7 Slice each cake in half horizontally with a serrated knife. Brush the cut sides with coffee liqueur. Put 1 cake layer cut-side up on a platter; spread with 1 cup frosting. Top with another cake layer, the coffee filling, another cake layer, the cocoa filling and the remaining cake layer. Frost the cake with the remaining frosting. Spread the ganache on top, letting it drip down. Let set 20 minutes.

This cake is inspired by sticky toffee pudding, the classic English dessert made with chopped dates and smothered in toffee sauce.

Gluten-Free Toffee Cake

ACTIVE: 40 min | TOTAL: 1 hr 40 min (plus cooling) | SERVES: 8 to 10

FOR THE CAKE

Cooking spray

8 ounces pitted dates, finely chopped

1½ cups water

½ teaspoon baking soda

1¾ cups oat flour

¾ cup almond flour

2 tablespoons cornstarch

¾ teaspoon ground cinnamon

½ teaspoon baking powder

½ teaspoon kosher salt

4 tablespoons unsalted butter, at room temperature

1 cup packed dark brown sugar

3 large eggs, at room temperature

2 teaspoons grated fresh ginger

1 teaspoon pure vanilla extract

FOR THE SAUCE

1 cup packed dark brown sugar

¾ cup heavy cream

1 stick unsalted butter

½ teaspoon pure vanilla extract

½ teaspoon kosher salt

Whipped cream, for serving

1 Make the cake: Preheat the oven to 325°. Coat an 8-inch square baking dish with cooking spray. Combine the dates and water in a medium saucepan and bring to a gentle simmer. Cook until the dates soften and the mixture is jam-like, about 5 minutes. Remove from the heat, stir in the baking soda and let cool to room temperature.

2 Whisk together the oat flour, almond flour, cornstarch, cinnamon, baking powder and salt in a medium bowl. Beat the butter in a large bowl with a mixer on medium-high speed until light and smooth, about 3 minutes. Add the brown sugar and beat until fully combined, about 4 minutes. Reduce the mixer speed to low and beat in the eggs until just combined, scraping down the bowl with a rubber spatula as necessary.

3 With a rubber spatula, fold the dry ingredients into the egg mixture until just combined. Fold in the cooled date mixture, ginger and vanilla. Pour the batter into the baking dish and gently tap against the counter to remove any air bubbles. Bake until a toothpick inserted into the center comes out clean, about 1 hour. Transfer the pan to a rack to cool completely.

4 Make the sauce: Combine the brown sugar, heavy cream, butter, vanilla and salt in a small saucepan. Bring to a boil over medium heat and cook, stirring, until the butter is melted. Reduce the heat to low and simmer, stirring, until the mixture is thick enough to coat a spoon, about 6 minutes. Let cool slightly.

5 Slice the cake into squares. Top each square with the sauce and whipped cream.

To get this look, pile the chocolate-swirled meringue on top of your cake, then use the back of a spoon to make swoops and peaks.

Towering Flourless Chocolate Cake

ACTIVE: 50 min I TOTAL: 1 hr 25 min (plus cooling) I SERVES: 8 to 10

FOR THE CAKE

2½ sticks unsalted butter, cut into pieces, plus more for the pan

6 ounces bittersweet chocolate, chopped

6 ounces unsweetened chocolate, chopped

6 large eggs

¾ cup turbinado or light brown sugar

Pinch of salt

½ cup stout beer (such as Guinness)

1 teaspoon pure vanilla extract

FOR THE MERINGUE

2 ounces semisweet chocolate, chopped

2 tablespoons unsalted butter

1 tablespoon light corn syrup

1 cup granulated sugar

3 large egg whites

¼ teaspoon cream of tartar

Pinch of salt

⅓ cup water

2 teaspoons pure vanilla extract

1 Make the cake: Preheat the oven to 325°. Butter the bottom and sides of a 9-inch springform pan and line the bottom with parchment paper. Put the bittersweet and unsweetened chocolate in a heatproof bowl and set over a saucepan of simmering water (do not let the bowl touch the water). Stir until the chocolate melts, then remove the bowl from the pan.

2 Put the eggs, turbinado sugar and salt in the bowl of a stand mixer. Set the bowl over the same pan of simmering water and whisk until the mixture is warm, about 2 minutes. Transfer the bowl to the stand mixer; beat with the whisk attachment on medium speed until tripled in volume, about 5 minutes.

3 Bring the beer and vanilla to a low boil in a saucepan. Reduce the mixer speed to low; beat in the beer mixture, then the melted chocolate, until combined, about 2 minutes. Gradually beat in the butter until combined.

4 Pour the batter into the prepared pan. Bake until a toothpick inserted into the center comes out with a few crumbs, about 35 minutes. Transfer to a rack and let cool 1 hour in the pan. Run a knife around the edge of the pan and remove the springform ring; let cool completely.

5 Make the meringue: Combine the chocolate, butter and corn syrup in a microwave-safe bowl. Microwave in 30-second intervals, stirring, until the chocolate is melted. Whisk together the granulated sugar, egg whites, cream of tartar, salt and water in a heatproof bowl. Put the bowl over a saucepan of simmering water (do net let the bowl touch the water); beat with a handheld mixer on low speed, then beat the mixture on high speed until soft peaks form, 5 minutes. Remove the bowl from the pan; beat until the meringue is cool and fluffy. Fold in the vanilla, then the melted chocolate, until swirled. Spread the meringue on the cake.

For maximum glaze coverage, cut the cake into squares, arrange on a rack set over a baking sheet and drizzle the glaze over each square, letting it drip down the sides.

Glazed Raspberry Crumb Cake

ACTIVE: 30 min **I** TOTAL: 1½ hr (plus cooling) **I** SERVES: 10 to 12

FOR THE CAKE

- 1 stick unsalted butter, at room temperature, plus more for the pan
- 2 cups all-purpose flour
- 1 teaspoon baking powder
- 1 teaspoon ground ginger
- ½ teaspoon kosher salt
- ½ teaspoon baking soda
- ¼ teaspoon freshly grated nutmeg
- 1 cup granulated sugar
- 2 large eggs
- 2 teaspoons pure vanilla extract
- 1 cup sour cream
- 2 cups fresh raspberries
- 1 cup raspberry jam

FOR THE CRUMB TOPPING

- 1¼ cups packed light brown sugar
- 1 cup all-purpose flour
- ½ cup rolled oats
- ½ teaspoon ground ginger
- ¼ teaspoon kosher salt
- 1 stick plus 2 tablespoons unsalted butter, cut into pieces, at room temperature

FOR THE GLAZE

- 1½ cups confectioners' sugar, sifted
- 3 to 4 tablespoons fresh lemon juice

1 Make the cake: Preheat the oven to 350°. Butter a 9-by-13-inch baking dish and line with parchment paper, leaving an overhang on the long sides. Whisk the flour, baking powder, ginger, salt, baking soda and nutmeg in a medium bowl.

2 Beat the butter and granulated sugar in a large bowl with a mixer on medium-high speed until light and fluffy, about 2 minutes. Add the eggs, one at a time, scraping down the sides of the bowl in between, and beat until combined. Mix in the vanilla. Reduce the mixer speed to low; add the flour mixture in 3 additions, alternating with the sour cream, beginning and ending with the flour. Beat on high speed for a few seconds just until smooth. Spread the batter in the baking dish.

3 Arrange the raspberries evenly over the batter, pressing them in. Dollop the jam in the empty spaces, then gently smooth with a spoon so the surface is evenly covered with jam and raspberries.

4 Make the crumb topping: Stir the brown sugar, flour, oats, ginger and salt in a medium bowl. Add the butter and work it in with your fingers to form a sandy mixture with small to medium clumps. Sprinkle evenly over the raspberry layer. Bake until puffed and set and a toothpick inserted into the center comes out with a few crumbs and a little bit of jam, 50 minutes to 1 hour. Transfer to a rack and let cool completely in the pan. Remove from the pan using the parchment overhang and cut into squares.

5 Make the glaze: Put the confectioners' sugar in a medium bowl; add the lemon juice, 1 tablespoon at a time, until the glaze is a thin consistency. Drizzle over the cake and let set.

Put a shallow baking dish of water on the lower oven rack and bake your cheesecake on the middle rack. The water will create steam and keep your cheesecake from cracking.

Triple Chocolate Cheesecake

ACTIVE: 30 min | TOTAL: 1 hr 45 min (plus chilling) | SERVES: 10 to 12

FOR THE CRUST

- 6 tablespoons unsalted butter, plus more for the pan
- 2 ounces semisweet chocolate, chopped
- ⅓ cup sugar
- 2 large eggs
- ⅔ cup all-purpose flour
- 2 tablespoons unsweetened cocoa powder
- ¼ teaspoon baking powder
- Pinch of salt

FOR THE FILLING

- 8 ounces milk chocolate, chopped
- 1 cup heavy cream
- 3 8-ounce packages cream cheese, at room temperature
- 1 cup sugar
- 3 large eggs
- 1 tablespoon pure vanilla extract
- 2 ounces white chocolate, for topping

1 Make the crust: Position racks in the middle and lower third of the oven; preheat to 325°. Butter the bottom and side of a 9-inch springform pan; wrap the outside of the pan with foil to catch any drips. Melt the butter and semisweet chocolate in a small saucepan over medium heat, stirring; remove from the heat and let cool slightly. Stir in the sugar and eggs until combined. Stir in the flour, cocoa powder, baking powder and salt until smooth and shiny. Spread in the prepared pan and bake until the top is set and no longer shiny, 10 to 15 minutes. Transfer to a rack to cool.

2 Make the filling: Fill a shallow baking dish halfway with water and set on the lower oven rack. Combine the milk chocolate and ½ cup heavy cream in a medium microwave-safe bowl. Microwave in 30-second intervals, stirring, until melted and smooth; set aside. Beat the cream cheese and sugar in a large bowl with a mixer on medium-high speed until smooth and fluffy, about 2 minutes. Reduce the mixer speed to low and beat in the eggs, one at a time, until just combined. Beat in the remaining ½ cup heavy cream and the vanilla. Add the melted chocolate mixture in 2 batches, beating until just combined. Stir a few times with a rubber spatula to make sure the chocolate is combined.

3 Pour the filling over the crust. Bake on the middle oven rack (directly over the baking dish of water) until the cheesecake is puffed and the edge is set, about 1 hour 15 minutes. (The center will still be very jiggly.) Transfer to a rack and let cool to room temperature, then cover with plastic wrap and refrigerate until cold and set, at least 6 hours or overnight.

4 Remove the cheesecake from the refrigerator about 1 hour before serving. Run a thin knife or offset spatula around the edge of the pan and remove the springform ring. Grate half of the white chocolate over the cheesecake, then use a vegetable peeler to shave the rest on top. Run a knife under hot water and dry well before slicing the cake.

Grate your carrots on the large holes of a box grater. Avoid pre-shredded carrots; they're too thick for carrot cake.

Carrot Cake with Orange Marmalade

ACTIVE: 1 hr **I** TOTAL: 2½ hr (plus cooling) **I** SERVES: 10 to 12

FOR THE CAKE

¾ cup vegetable oil, plus more for the pans

1 cup pecan halves

2 cups all-purpose flour

2 teaspoons baking powder

1½ teaspoons baking soda

1 teaspoon salt

2 teaspoons ground cinnamon

1 teaspoon ground ginger

¾ cup granulated sugar

1 teaspoon finely grated lemon zest

4 large eggs

½ cup plus 3 tablespoons orange marmalade, plus more for topping

3 cups shredded carrots (about ¾ pound carrots)

FOR THE FROSTING

3 8-ounce packages cream cheese, at room temperature

12 tablespoons (1½ sticks) unsalted butter, at room temperature

3 cups confectioners' sugar

1 tablespoon fresh lemon juice

1 tablespoon pure vanilla extract

Pinch of salt

1 Make the cake: Position racks in the upper and lower thirds of the oven and preheat to 350˚. Brush three 9-inch round cake pans with vegetable oil and line the bottoms with parchment paper. Spread the pecans on a baking sheet and bake until toasted, about 10 minutes. Let cool, then pulse in a food processor until very finely chopped.

2 Combine the pecans, flour, baking powder, baking soda, salt, cinnamon, ginger and granulated sugar in a large bowl. In another large bowl, whisk together the vegetable oil, lemon zest, eggs and ½ cup marmalade. Stir in the carrots, then fold the carrot mixture into the flour mixture until just combined. Divide the batter among the cake pans and spread evenly (it won't look like a lot of batter, but the cakes will rise in the oven). Put 2 pans on the upper oven rack and the third pan on the lower rack. Bake, switching the position of the pans halfway through, until the cakes bounce back when touched and a toothpick inserted into the centers comes out clean, 20 to 25 minutes. Transfer the pans to racks until cool enough to handle, then invert the cakes onto the racks to cool completely; discard the parchment.

3 Make the frosting: Beat the cream cheese and butter in a bowl with a mixer until smooth, scraping down the bowl as needed. Beat in the confectioners' sugar, lemon juice, vanilla and salt until smooth.

4 Put 1 cake layer on a cake stand or platter. Spread 1 tablespoon marmalade on top, then spread about ¾ cup frosting over the marmalade. Top with another cake layer, then more marmalade and frosting. Add the final cake layer, then cover the whole cake with a thin layer of frosting (this is the crumb coat; it doesn't have to be perfect). Refrigerate 1 hour, then cover with the remaining frosting. Swirl some marmalade into the top of the cake. Refrigerate until ready to serve.

This cake gets its heat from guajillo chiles, which are dried peppers with a slightly fruity, smoky flavor.

Spicy Texas Sheet Cake

ACTIVE: 1 hr **|** TOTAL: 1 hr 45 min (plus cooling) **|** SERVES: 12

FOR THE CAKE

- 2 sticks unsalted butter, plus more for the pan
- 2 dried guajillo chile peppers, stems removed
- 1 cup water
- 2 cups all-purpose flour
- 1 cup granulated sugar
- ⅔ cup packed dark brown sugar
- ½ teaspoon salt
- ½ teaspoon baking powder
- ¼ cup unsweetened cocoa powder
- ½ cup buttermilk
- 2 large eggs
- 2 teaspoons pure vanilla extract
- 1 teaspoon baking soda

FOR THE FROSTING

- 1½ cups chopped pecans
- 1½ sticks (12 tablespoons) unsalted butter
- ½ teaspoon cayenne pepper

Pinch of salt

- 2 tablespoons unsweetened cocoa powder
- 3 cups confectioners' sugar
- ⅓ cup whole milk

1 Make the cake: Preheat the oven to 350°. Line a 9-by-13-inch baking dish with parchment paper, leaving a 2-inch overhang on 2 sides; butter the parchment. Toast the chiles in a dry medium saucepan over medium heat until darkened and pliable, about 5 minutes. Remove from the heat, add the water and let soak until the chiles soften, about 5 more minutes. Transfer the chiles and soaking liquid to a blender and puree. Strain through a fine-mesh sieve back into the saucepan. Finely chop any chile pieces left in the sieve and add to the saucepan.

2 Whisk together the flour, granulated sugar, brown sugar, salt and baking powder in a large bowl. Add the butter and cocoa powder to the saucepan with the chile puree; bring to a boil over medium heat, stirring, until the butter is melted. Pour into the flour mixture and stir until combined. Whisk together the buttermilk, eggs, vanilla and baking soda in a liquid measuring cup; add to the batter in 2 additions, stirring until combined.

3 Pour the batter into the baking dish, spreading it evenly. Bake until a toothpick inserted into the center comes out clean, about 35 minutes. Transfer to a rack and let cool slightly in the pan.

4 Meanwhile, make the frosting: Combine the pecans, butter, cayenne and salt in a medium saucepan. Cook over medium heat until the butter is melted and the pecans are toasted, about 5 minutes. Remove ½ cup pecans with a slotted spoon and set aside for topping. Stir the cocoa powder into the saucepan and remove from the heat. Whisk in the confectioners' sugar in 2 batches, alternating with the milk, mixing well.

5 Immediately pour the warm frosting over the warm cake and gently spread to cover with an offset spatula. Top with the reserved pecans and let cool completely before slicing.

Pies & Tarts

Banana Pudding Tart

ACTIVE: 45 min I TOTAL: 1 hr (plus 2 hr chilling) I SERVES: 8

FOR THE CRUST

60 vanilla wafer cookies
    (from an 11-ounce box)
2   tablespoons sugar
4   tablespoons unsalted
    butter, melted

FOR THE FILLING AND TOPPING

½   cup whole milk
½   cup heavy cream
¾   cup sugar, plus more
    for sprinkling
2   large eggs, separated
2   tablespoons cornstarch
⅛   teaspoon kosher salt
1   tablespoon unsalted butter
1   teaspoon pure vanilla
    extract
4 to 5 large bananas
¼   teaspoon cream of tartar

When making
a pudding pie or
tart like this one,
press a piece of plastic
wrap on the surface
before refrigerating to
keep a skin from
forming.

1 Make the crust: Preheat the oven to 350°. Place the cookies and sugar in a food processor and process until finely ground. Add the melted butter and process until it looks like wet sand. Transfer to a 9½-inch fluted tart pan and press into the bottom and up the sides. Bake until golden brown, about 12 minutes. Transfer to a rack and let cool completely.

2 Make the filling: Set a large fine-mesh sieve over a medium bowl. Combine the milk, heavy cream, ¼ cup sugar, the egg yolks, cornstarch and salt in a medium saucepan; whisk until smooth. Place the saucepan over medium heat and cook, whisking constantly, until the mixture bubbles, about 5 minutes. Reduce the heat to low and continue cooking for 1 minute, whisking. Remove from the heat and immediately transfer to the sieve; press through with a rubber spatula. Stir in the butter and vanilla. Let cool to room temperature, stirring occasionally.

3 Peel and thinly slice 2 bananas and arrange evenly on the bottom of the crust. Gently spread the filling on top of the bananas and smooth the surface. Press a piece of plastic wrap directly on the surface; refrigerate until set, 2 hours.

4 Peel and thinly slice the remaining bananas and arrange them on the tart, overlapping the slices. Sprinkle with sugar and brown with a kitchen torch.

5 Make the topping: Bring a few inches of water to a simmer in a medium saucepan over medium heat. Whisk the egg whites, remaining ½ cup sugar and the cream of tartar in a large heatproof bowl. Set the bowl over the saucepan (do not let the bowl touch the water); cook, whisking, until the sugar dissolves, the egg whites are frothy and the mixture is warm, 3 to 5 minutes. Remove the bowl from the pan and beat with a mixer on medium-high speed until the meringue is cool and stiff peaks form, about 5 minutes. Transfer to a piping bag; pipe the meringue around the edge of the tart. Brown with the kitchen torch.

If you don't have a kitchen torch, you can toast the meringue under the broiler. Just keep an eye on it so it doesn't burn!

Mile-High S'mores Pie

ACTIVE: 50 min **|** TOTAL: 50 min (plus 3 hr chilling) **|** SERVES: 8 to 10

FOR THE CRUST

1½ cups graham cracker crumbs (from 10 to 12 whole crackers)

3 tablespoons sugar

6 tablespoons unsalted butter, melted

FOR THE FILLING

2 cups whole milk

4 large egg yolks

½ cup sugar

3 tablespoons cornstarch

¼ teaspoon salt

8 ounces milk chocolate, finely chopped

2 tablespoons unsalted butter

FOR THE MERINGUE

5 large egg whites

¾ cup sugar

¼ teaspoon cream of tartar

Pinch of salt

¼ teaspoon pure vanilla extract

1 Make the crust: Preheat the oven to 350°. Mix the graham cracker crumbs, sugar and melted butter in a medium bowl until combined. Press evenly into the bottom and up the sides of a 9-inch pie plate. Bake until lightly toasted, about 10 minutes; set aside to cool.

2 Make the filling: Heat the milk in a medium saucepan over medium heat until almost simmering. Whisk the egg yolks, sugar, cornstarch and salt in a medium bowl to make a thick paste. Whisk about one-third of the warm milk into the egg mixture until smooth. Add this mixture to the remaining milk in the saucepan and cook, whisking constantly, until it starts to bubble and thicken, about 2 minutes. Continue cooking, whisking, until thick like pudding, 1 to 2 more minutes.

3 Remove the pan from the heat and whisk in the chocolate until melted and combined. Whisk in the butter until combined. Pour the filling into the graham cracker crust and refrigerate until completely cool, about 2 hours.

4 Make the meringue: Whisk the egg whites, sugar, cream of tartar and salt in a large heatproof bowl (or the bowl of a stand mixer) until combined. Set the bowl over a medium saucepan with 1 inch of simmering water (don't let the bowl touch the water). Cook, whisking constantly, until the mixture is just hot to the touch and the sugar is completely dissolved, 3 to 4 minutes.

5 Remove the bowl from the saucepan. Add the vanilla. Beat with a mixer on medium-high speed until stiff glossy peaks form, 4 to 5 minutes. Transfer the meringue to a piping bag fitted with a ¾-inch-wide tip. Pipe large marshmallow-size mounds on the surface of the pie, leaving a small border of the filling exposed. Pipe another layer of mounds on top in a slightly smaller circle, then pipe a third layer on top, using the rest of the meringue. Use a kitchen torch to toast the meringue. Refrigerate the pie until cooled before slicing, at least 1 hour.

PB&J Tart

ACTIVE: 25 min **I** TOTAL: 1½ hr (plus cooling) **I** SERVES: 10 to 12

1½ sticks (12 tablespoons)
   unsalted butter,
   at room temperature,
   plus more for the pan

2¼ cups all-purpose flour

½ teaspoon baking powder

¼ teaspoon salt

1 cup peanut butter
   (creamy or crunchy)

½ cup granulated sugar

¾ cup confectioners' sugar

1 large egg

1 teaspoon pure vanilla
   extract

½ cup strawberry jam

1 Preheat the oven to 350°. Generously butter a 9-inch fluted tart pan with a removable bottom.

2 Whisk the flour, baking powder and salt in a medium bowl. Beat the butter, peanut butter and both sugars in another bowl with a mixer until smooth. Beat in the egg and vanilla. Add the flour mixture and stir with a wooden spoon to combine.

3 Press half of the dough into the bottom and up the sides of the tart pan. Spread the strawberry jam over the dough, leaving a ½-inch border around the edge. Drop about half of the remaining dough over the jam by the tablespoonful; lightly press the rest of the dough into the pan around the edges to form a rim. Bake until golden, 45 to 50 minutes. Transfer to a rack and let cool completely in the pan.

You can also use this recipe to make bar cookies. Just press half of the dough into an oiled foil-lined 8-inch square baking dish, then continue as directed.

Puff Pastry Berry Cheesecake Tart

ACTIVE: 25 min **I** TOTAL: 45 min (plus cooling) **I** SERVES: 8

3 cups mixed strawberries, blackberries, blueberries and raspberries (halve or quarter the strawberries)
⅓ cup plus 1 teaspoon sugar
All-purpose flour, for dusting
1 sheet frozen puff pastry (half of a 17-ounce package), thawed
6 ounces cream cheese, at room temperature
2 tablespoons heavy cream

You should thaw frozen puff pastry overnight in the fridge. If you're short on time you can thaw it at room temperature, but don't microwave it!

1 Preheat the oven to 400°. Gently toss the berries with 1 teaspoon sugar in a large bowl. Set aside while you prepare the crust.

2 On a lightly floured surface, roll out the puff pastry into a 10-by-12-inch rectangle. Cut a ½-inch-thick strip off each side with a sharp knife. Lay the strips on top of the edges of the pastry to create a rim around the tart. Carefully transfer the pastry shell to a baking sheet and prick the center all over with a fork.

3 Bake the crust until golden brown, about 20 minutes. Transfer to a rack and let cool completely.

4 Meanwhile, beat the cream cheese with the heavy cream and remaining ⅓ cup sugar in a large bowl with a mixer on medium speed until fully combined. Spread the cream cheese mixture evenly on the cooled crust. Top with the berries.

Brushing your crust with egg wash before baking gives it a nice golden brown sheen. The egg also helps any toppings, like sugar or nuts, stick to the crust.

Grape Galette with Almond Cream

ACTIVE: 45 min I TOTAL: 2 hr 25 min (plus cooling) I SERVES: 8

FOR THE CRUST

- 1¾ cups all-purpose flour, plus more for dusting
- 5 tablespoons sugar
- 1 teaspoon salt
- 10 tablespoons cold unsalted butter, cut into small pieces
- ¼ cup ice water, plus 1 tablespoon water for the egg wash
- 1 large egg yolk, for the egg wash

FOR THE FILLING

- ½ cup plus 2 tablespoons sliced almonds
- ¼ cup plus 2 tablespoons sugar
- 1 large egg yolk
- 2 tablespoons unsalted butter, at room temperature
- 1½ teaspoons pure vanilla extract
- 1 teaspoon finely grated lemon zest
- 1 pound assorted seedless grapes (about 2 cups)

1 Make the crust: Pulse the flour, sugar and salt in a food processor. Add half of the butter and pulse until the mixture looks like coarse meal. Add the remaining butter and pulse into pea-size pieces. Add ¼ cup ice water; pulse until the dough clumps together but has not yet formed a ball. Turn out the dough onto a piece of plastic wrap, press into a disk and wrap. Refrigerate until firm, at least 1 hour or overnight.

2 Meanwhile, make the filling: Combine ½ cup almonds, ¼ cup sugar, the egg yolk, butter, vanilla and lemon zest in a food processor. Pulse to make a paste.

3 Preheat the oven to 400° and line a baking sheet with parchment paper. Roll out the dough into a 12-inch round on a lightly floured surface. Transfer the dough to the baking sheet. Spread the almond filling over the dough, leaving a 2½-inch border; top with the grapes. Fold the edge of the dough over the fruit by about 2 inches, pleating as needed. Refrigerate until firm, 30 minutes.

4 Lightly beat the remaining egg yolk and 1 tablespoon water. Brush the dough with the egg wash. Scatter the remaining 2 tablespoons almonds all over the galette, then sprinkle with the remaining 2 tablespoons sugar. Bake until the crust is golden brown and the grapes are softened, about 40 minutes. Let cool on the baking sheet.

It's a good idea to bake fruit pies on a preheated baking sheet. The extra heat helps cook the bottom crust and keep it from getting soggy.

Cinnamon Bun Apple Pie

ACTIVE: 25 min | TOTAL: 1 hr 15 min (plus cooling) | SERVES: 6 to 8

1 14-ounce package refrigerated pie dough (2 rounds)

All-purpose flour, for dusting

2 tablespoons unsalted butter, at room temperature

½ cup granulated sugar

1⅛ teaspoons ground cinnamon

5 assorted apples, such as McIntosh, Granny Smith and Pink Lady (about 2 pounds)

Juice of 1 lemon

1 teaspoon pure vanilla extract

1 large egg, lightly beaten

⅔ cup confectioners' sugar

2 tablespoons milk, plus more if needed

1 Place a baking sheet in the oven and preheat to 400°. Line a 9-inch pie plate with 1 piece of pie dough; refrigerate until ready to assemble.

2 Make the cinnamon-roll crust: Unroll the remaining piece of pie dough on a lightly floured surface and spread the butter evenly on top. Combine ¼ cup granulated sugar and 1 teaspoon cinnamon in a small bowl; sprinkle evenly over the butter, then gently press with your fingers to help the mixture adhere. Roll the pie dough into a tight log. Trim and discard about 1½ inches from both ends; cut the remaining log crosswise into ½-inch-thick pieces. Arrange the pieces cut-side down in a snug circle on floured parchment paper. Lightly dust with more flour, then gently roll out into a 10-inch round. Slide the parchment onto a baking sheet and refrigerate until ready to assemble the pie.

3 Peel and thinly slice the apples. Toss with the lemon juice, vanilla and the remaining ¼ cup granulated sugar and ⅛ teaspoon cinnamon in a large bowl. Spoon into the dough-lined pie plate; invert the cinnamon-roll crust on top and peel off the parchment (it's OK if the individual rounds separate a bit in the process). Pinch the edges of the crusts together; fold the overhanging dough under itself and crimp. Brush with the beaten egg.

4 Set the pie on the hot baking sheet in the oven; bake until the crust is golden brown and the filling is bubbling, about 50 minutes. (Tent loosely with foil if the top is browning too quickly.) Transfer to a rack to cool slightly.

5 Whisk the confectioners' sugar and 2 tablespoons milk in a medium bowl until smooth; add more milk if the glaze is too thick. Drizzle over the pie.

Don't worry if your crust tears when you transfer it to the tart pan; you can just press it back together.

Chocolate-Toffee Pecan Tart

ACTIVE: 50 min **I** TOTAL: 4 hr (plus cooling) **I** SERVES: 6 to 8

FOR THE CRUST

- 1 cup all-purpose flour, plus more for dusting
- ½ cup dutch-process cocoa powder
- ½ cup confectioners' sugar
- ¼ teaspoon fine salt
- 1 stick cold unsalted butter, cut into ½-inch pieces
- 1 large egg, beaten

FOR THE FILLING

- 1½ cups pecan halves
- 10 tablespoons unsalted butter
- 6 tablespoons granulated sugar
- 1 teaspoon pure vanilla extract
- ¼ teaspoon kosher salt
- ⅔ cup light corn syrup
- ¼ cup packed dark brown sugar
- 3 large eggs, beaten
- 3 tablespoons bourbon

1 Make the crust: Pulse the flour, cocoa powder, confectioners' sugar and fine salt in a food processor until combined. Add the butter; pulse until the mixture looks like coarse meal with pea-size bits of butter. Add the egg and pulse once or twice. (Stop before the dough gathers into a ball.) Turn out onto a sheet of plastic wrap and press into a disk. Wrap tightly and refrigerate until firm, at least 1 hour.

2 Place the dough on a large sheet of lightly floured parchment paper. Roll out into a 12-inch round, no more than ⅛ inch thick. Invert the dough into a 9-inch tart pan with a removable bottom and peel off the parchment; press the dough into the bottom and sides of the pan. Trim the excess dough. Cover with plastic wrap and refrigerate at least 1 hour.

3 Position racks in the middle and lower third of the oven; preheat to 350˚. Line the crust with foil, then fill with pie weights or dried beans. Bake on the middle rack, 20 minutes. Remove the foil and weights and continue baking until crisp, 7 to 10 minutes. Transfer to a rack to cool completely.

4 Make the filling: Coarsely chop 1 cup pecans. Combine the butter, granulated sugar, vanilla and kosher salt in a saucepan; bring to a boil over medium-high heat. Cook, stirring, until the mixture turns dark amber, 6 to 8 minutes. Stir in the chopped pecans and cook 1 to 2 more minutes. Remove from the heat and whisk in the corn syrup and brown sugar until dissolved. Let cool until lukewarm, then whisk in the eggs and bourbon until combined.

5 Increase the oven temperature to 375˚. Place the tart shell on a baking sheet and pour in the filling up to the brim. Arrange the remaining ½ cup pecan halves on top. Bake on the lower oven rack until the tart is evenly browned and slightly domed in the center, about 40 minutes. Transfer to a rack to cool completely.

You can make this poppy seed tart in a standard 9-inch pie dish. No need to adjust the recipe!

Poppy Seed Tart

ACTIVE: 45 min I TOTAL: 2 hr (plus 5 hr chilling) I SERVES: 8 to 10

FOR THE CRUST

1¼ cups all-purpose flour,
    plus more for dusting

¼ cup sugar

1 teaspoon finely grated
    lemon zest

¼ teaspoon salt

1 stick cold unsalted butter,
    cut into ½-inch pieces

1 large egg yolk

2 tablespoons ice water

Cooking spray

FOR THE FILLING

½ cup sugar

4 large egg yolks

3 tablespoons cornstarch

Pinch of salt

1½ cups whole milk

2 tablespoons unsalted
    butter

1 teaspoon pure vanilla
    extract

½ cup cold heavy cream

1 tablespoon poppy seeds

1 Make the crust: Pulse the flour, sugar, lemon zest and salt in a food processor. Add the butter and pulse until the mixture looks like coarse meal. Add the egg yolk and ice water; pulse until the dough begins to come together. Turn out onto a sheet of plastic wrap and pat into a disk. Wrap tightly and refrigerate until firm, at least 1 hour and up to 1 day.

2 Lightly coat a 9-inch tart pan with a removable bottom with cooking spray. Roll out the dough into a 10-inch round on a lightly floured surface. (If it gets too soft, return to the refrigerator until firm.) Ease the dough into the tart pan and press into the bottom and up the sides, trimming any excess. Pierce the bottom all over with a fork. Refrigerate until firm, at least 1 hour or overnight.

3 Preheat the oven to 375°. Put the tart pan on a baking sheet. Line the crust with foil, then fill with pie weights or dried beans. Transfer the baking sheet to the oven; bake until the crust edges are golden, about 20 minutes. Remove the foil and weights and continue baking until the crust is golden all over, 15 to 20 more minutes. Transfer to a rack to cool completely.

4 Meanwhile, make the filling: Whisk the sugar, egg yolks, cornstarch and salt in a bowl until combined. Heat the milk in a small saucepan over medium heat (do not boil). Gradually whisk half of the hot milk into the egg mixture, then pour back into the saucepan with the remaining milk and cook, whisking, until thick like pudding, 4 minutes. Whisk in the butter and vanilla. Pour the filling through a fine-mesh sieve into a large bowl. Let cool to room temperature, stirring frequently, about 30 minutes.

5 Beat the heavy cream in a large bowl with a mixer until soft peaks form. Gently fold the whipped cream and poppy seeds into the cooled filling. Spoon into the cooled crust and smooth the top. Cover loosely with plastic wrap and refrigerate until set, at least 3 hours or overnight.

Peach Custard Pie

ACTIVE: 45 min I TOTAL: 3 hr 35 min (plus cooling and chilling) I SERVES: 8 to 10

FOR THE CRUST

1¼ cups all-purpose flour, plus more for dusting

1 tablespoon granulated sugar

½ teaspoon kosher salt

1 stick cold unsalted butter, diced

½ teaspoon distilled white vinegar

2 to 3 tablespoons ice water

FOR THE FILLING

¾ cup granulated sugar

3 tablespoons all-purpose flour

Pinch of kosher salt

½ cup heavy cream

½ cup sour cream

3 large eggs

1½ teaspoons vanilla bean paste

1 pound ripe peaches (3 to 4), pitted and cut into ½-inch-thick wedges

Confectioners' sugar, for dusting

1 Make the crust: Pulse the flour, granulated sugar and salt in a food processor a few times to combine. Add the butter and pulse until pea-size pieces form. Combine the vinegar with 1 tablespoon ice water, then drizzle into the food processor with the motor running. Continue adding up to 2 more tablespoons ice water, 1 teaspoon at a time, pulsing, until the dough comes together. Pat the dough into a disk and wrap tightly in plastic wrap. Refrigerate until firm, at least 1 hour or overnight.

2 Remove the dough from the refrigerator and let it soften slightly, 10 to 15 minutes. Roll out the dough on a lightly floured surface into an 11- to 12-inch round. Ease into a 9-inch pie plate. Fold in the overhanging dough and crimp as desired. Refrigerate at least 30 minutes.

3 Preheat the oven to 425°. Line the dough with parchment paper and fill with pie weights or dried beans. Bake until the edges of the crust are just golden, about 15 minutes. Remove the parchment and weights; continue baking until the bottom of the crust is dry, 5 to 10 more minutes.

4 Reduce the oven temperature to 350°. Make the filling: Whisk the granulated sugar, flour and salt in a large bowl. In a separate bowl, whisk the heavy cream, sour cream, eggs and vanilla paste, then add to the dry ingredients and whisk until smooth.

5 Arrange the peaches in the crust in an even layer, then pour in the custard filling. Once the oven has cooled to 350°, bake the pie until the custard is set but slightly jiggly in the center, 50 to 55 minutes. Transfer to a rack and let cool completely, then refrigerate until chilled. Dust with confectioners' sugar before serving.

When baking custard pies like this one, take the pie out of the oven when it looks set but still jiggles a bit in the center. It will continue to set as it cools and chills.

Sugar Cream Pie

ACTIVE: 35 min I TOTAL: 3 hr 10 min (plus cooling) I SERVES: 8 to 10

FOR THE CRUST

- 1¼ cups all-purpose flour, plus more for dusting
- ½ teaspoon salt
- 6 tablespoons cold unsalted butter, cut into ½-inch pieces
- 2 tablespoons cold vegetable shortening
- 3 to 4 tablespoons ice water

FOR THE FILLING

- 2 cups heavy cream
- 1 cup sugar
- ½ cup all-purpose flour
- ½ teaspoon pure vanilla extract
- 2 tablespoons unsalted butter, cut into ½-inch pieces
- ⅛ teaspoon freshly grated nutmeg

1 Make the crust: Pulse the flour and salt in a food processor. Add the butter and shortening and pulse until the mixture looks like coarse meal with pea-size bits of butter. Drizzle in 3 tablespoons ice water and pulse until the dough begins to come together (add more water, ½ tablespoon at a time, if necessary). Turn out onto a sheet of plastic wrap and pat into a disk; wrap tightly and refrigerate at least 1 hour and up to 1 day.

2 Roll out the dough into an 11-inch round on a lightly floured surface. Ease into a 9-inch pie plate. Fold the overhanging dough under itself and crimp the edges with your fingers. Pierce the bottom all over with a fork. Refrigerate the crust until firm, about 30 minutes.

3 Make the filling: Place a baking sheet on the middle oven rack and preheat to 425°. Whisk the heavy cream, sugar, flour and vanilla in a bowl. Pour into the chilled crust, dot with the butter and sprinkle the nutmeg on top. Carefully transfer the pie plate to the hot baking sheet and bake 10 minutes. Reduce the oven temperature to 350° and continue baking until the crust is golden and the filling is bubbly in spots, about 55 more minutes (the center will still jiggle slightly); cover the crust edges with foil if they're browning too quickly. Transfer to a rack to cool completely. Serve chilled or at room temperature.

This pie is often called Hoosier Pie because it's so beloved in Indiana (the Hoosier State). It was even declared the official state pie!

A slab pie is a great choice for a crowd. You can make this one in a jelly roll pan or on a rimmed baking sheet.

Spiced Cherry-Berry Slab Pie

ACTIVE: 50 min | TOTAL: 3 hr (plus cooling) | SERVES: 12 to 16

FOR THE CRUST

2½ cups all-purpose flour,
    plus more for dusting

2 tablespoons granulated sugar

1 teaspoon salt

¼ cup cold vegetable shortening

1½ sticks (12 tablespoons)
    cold unsalted butter,
    cut into small cubes

3 tablespoons apple cider
    vinegar

6 to 8 tablespoons ice water

FOR THE TOPPING

1 cup all-purpose flour

⅓ cup packed light brown sugar

¼ teaspoon ground cinnamon

¼ teaspoon salt

1 stick unsalted butter,
    cut into small cubes,
    at room temperature

FOR THE FILLING

6 cups pitted cherries
    (about 2 pounds)

2 cups blueberries

2 cups chopped strawberries

1¼ cups granulated sugar

2 teaspoons pure vanilla extract

2 teaspoons white balsamic
    vinegar

¼ cup cornstarch

½ teaspoon freshly ground
    pepper

¼ teaspoon ground cinnamon

Pinch of salt

1 Make the crust: Pulse the flour, granulated sugar and salt in a food processor. Add the shortening and half the butter and pulse until just combined. Add the remaining butter and pulse a few times until pea-size pieces form. Drizzle in the cider vinegar and 6 tablespoons ice water; pulse just to combine. The dough should be crumbly but hold together when squeezed; if it doesn't, add up to 2 more tablespoons water, 1 teaspoon at a time. Turn out the dough onto a sheet of plastic wrap; press and knead a few times to combine. Wrap and press into an 8-inch square. Refrigerate at least 1 hour or overnight.

2 Make the topping: Stir together the flour, brown sugar, cinnamon and salt in a medium bowl. Add the butter and work it into the flour mixture with your fingers until crumbs form. Refrigerate until ready to use.

3 Put a baking sheet on the middle rack of the oven; preheat to 400°. Roll out the dough on a lightly floured surface into a 13-by-18-inch rectangle. (If the dough is too soft, refrigerate 10 to 20 minutes before continuing.) Ease into a 10-by-15-inch jelly roll pan or rimmed baking sheet; trim the excess dough so the edges are even. Refrigerate the crust until ready to fill.

4 Make the filling: Combine the cherries, blueberries, strawberries, granulated sugar, vanilla and balsamic vinegar in a large bowl. Toss until the sugar starts to dissolve. Set aside until slightly juicy, 15 to 20 minutes. Add the cornstarch, pepper, cinnamon and salt and toss until the cornstarch dissolves.

5 Spread the filling in the chilled crust. Evenly sprinkle the crumb topping all over. Set the pie on the hot baking sheet in the oven and bake until the edges and topping are deep golden brown and the filling is bubbling and thickened, about 1 hour. Transfer to a rack to cool completely.

A springform pan works best for high-sided tarts like this one. A tart pan is too shallow.

Pear-Walnut Chocolate Tart

ACTIVE: 1 hr I TOTAL: 3 hr (plus cooling) I SERVES: 8 to 10

FOR THE CRUST

1¼ cups all-purpose flour, plus more for dusting

3 tablespoons cold vegetable shortening

1 tablespoon granulated sugar

½ teaspoon salt

5 tablespoons cold unsalted butter, cut into small pieces

2 tablespoons ice water

FOR THE FILLING

1½ cups walnuts

6 tablespoons unsalted butter, cut into small pieces, at room temperature

1 cup confectioners' sugar

1 large egg

¼ teaspoon ground cinnamon

Pinch of salt

2 cups water

½ cup granulated sugar

1 large firm pear (such as Bosc, Bartlett or Anjou)

⅓ cup semisweet or milk chocolate chunks

1 Make the crust: Pulse the flour, shortening, granulated sugar and salt in a food processor until combined. Add the butter and pulse until it is in pea-size pieces. Drizzle in the ice water and pulse until the dough just comes together. Turn out onto a piece of plastic wrap and form the dough into a disk. Wrap and refrigerate until firm, at least 1 hour or overnight.

2 Roll out the dough into a 12-inch round on a lightly floured surface. Ease into a 9-inch springform pan, pressing it into the bottom and 2 inches up the sides. Refrigerate 30 minutes.

3 Preheat the oven to 350°. Line the crust with foil and fill with pie weights or dried beans. Bake until golden around the edge, about 20 minutes. Remove the foil and weights and continue baking until the crust is golden all over, 10 to 15 more minutes. Transfer to a rack to cool completely.

4 Meanwhile, make the filling: Spread the walnuts on a baking sheet. Toast in the oven, 8 to 10 minutes; let cool. Pulse in a food processor with the butter, confectioners' sugar, egg, cinnamon and salt to form a paste; set aside.

5 Combine the water and granulated sugar in a medium saucepan and bring to a simmer over medium-high heat. Peel the pear and cut into ¾-inch chunks. Add to the saucepan and simmer until tender, 8 to 10 minutes. Drain, then spread the pear on paper towels to cool completely.

6 Spread the walnut filling evenly in the cooled crust, then press the pear and chocolate chunks into the filling. Bake until the filling is puffed and golden and a toothpick inserted into the center comes out clean, 30 to 40 minutes. Transfer to a rack to cool completely.

Classic Lemon Tart

ACTIVE: 45 min I TOTAL: 45 min (plus 4 hr chilling) I SERVES: 8 to 10

FOR THE CRUST

14 whole graham crackers

2 tablespoons sugar

5 tablespoons unsalted
butter, melted

FOR THE LEMON CURD

1 cup sugar

1 tablespoon grated lemon
zest, plus ½ cup lemon
juice (from 2 to 3 lemons)

Pinch of salt

3 large eggs plus 3 egg yolks

4 tablespoons cold
unsalted butter,
cut into small pieces

Whipped cream, for topping

Lemon curd is
super easy to make.
You only need five
simple ingredients:
sugar, lemons, salt,
eggs and butter!

1 Make the crust: Preheat the oven to 350˚. Break the graham crackers into pieces, then pulse in a food processor with the sugar until finely ground. Drizzle in the melted butter and pulse to combine.

2 Press the crumb mixture into the bottom and about 1 inch up the sides of a 9-inch springform pan. Bake until golden, about 10 minutes, then transfer to a rack to cool completely.

3 Meanwhile, make the lemon curd: Whisk the sugar, lemon zest, lemon juice and salt in a medium saucepan. Whisk the whole eggs and yolks in a small bowl, then whisk into the lemon mixture. Cook the mixture over medium heat, whisking constantly, until it's thick like pudding, 6 to 8 minutes. Remove from the heat and whisk in the butter a few pieces at a time until combined.

4 Strain the curd through a fine-mesh sieve into a small bowl, pushing it through with a rubber spatula. Pour the curd into the cooled crust and gently press plastic wrap directly onto the surface to prevent a skin from forming. Refrigerate until set, at least 4 hours.

5 Remove the springform ring and transfer the tart to a platter. Top with whipped cream.

Peach Hand Pies

ACTIVE: 40 min | TOTAL: 1 hr 15 min (plus cooling) | MAKES: 6

6   peaches, peeled and chopped

½   cup water

½   vanilla bean, split and seeds
     scraped

¼   cup granulated sugar

2   tablespoons packed light
     brown sugar

2   teaspoons fresh lemon juice

Pinch of salt

1   14-ounce package refrigerated
     pie dough (2 rounds)

All-purpose flour, for dusting

1   large egg, beaten

1 Combine the peaches, water, vanilla bean (seeds and pod), granulated sugar, brown sugar, lemon juice and salt in a large saucepan. Bring to a simmer and cook until softened, 12 to 18 minutes. Discard the vanilla pod and mash the peaches; let the compote cool.

2 Preheat the oven to 425°. Line a baking sheet with parchment paper. Using your hands, press each round of pie dough into a small compact square. On a lightly floured surface, roll out each square with a rolling pin into a 12-inch square. Cut each square in half using a sharp knife or pastry cutter, then cut each half crosswise into thirds to make twelve 4-by-6-inch rectangles.

3 Arrange 6 rectangles on the baking sheet and top each with 3 tablespoons of the peach compote. Cover each with another rectangle of dough; crimp the edges with a fork. Cut a few small vents into the top of each hand pie and brush with the beaten egg. Bake until the hand pies are golden, 20 to 25 minutes. Let cool on the baking sheet.

To peel peaches
easily, blanch them
in boiling water for
about 30 seconds, then
remove to an ice bath.
The skins should
slip right off.

Use a light-colored pan when making caramel so you can see the color of the caramel as it cooks.

Dark Chocolate-Caramel Tart

ACTIVE: 1 hr I TOTAL: 2½ hr (plus 3 hr chilling) I SERVES: 8 to 10

FOR THE CRUST

1 cup all-purpose flour

⅓ cup unsweetened dutch-process cocoa powder

⅓ cup sugar

½ teaspoon fine sea salt

5 tablespoons plus 1 teaspoon cold unsalted butter, diced

1 large egg yolk

4 to 6 teaspoons ice water

FOR THE FILLING

1 cup sugar

6 tablespoons water

1 cup heavy cream

1 teaspoon pure vanilla extract

¾ teaspoon fine sea salt

6 ounces semisweet or bittersweet chocolate, chopped

1 stick unsalted butter, diced

5 large egg yolks plus 1 whole egg

Flaky sea salt

1 Make the crust: Combine the flour, cocoa powder, sugar and fine sea salt in a food processor; pulse to combine. Add the butter and pulse until the mixture looks like sand. Add the egg yolk and 4 teaspoons ice water; pulse until the dough comes together and forms a ball, adding up to 2 more teaspoons ice water if necessary. Press the dough into a 9-inch fluted tart pan in an even layer. Refrigerate at least 30 minutes.

2 Preheat the oven to 350°. Line the crust with parchment paper and fill with pie weights or dried beans. Bake until the crust looks dry, 13 to 15 minutes. Remove the paper and weights and bake 5 more minutes. Transfer the crust to a rack to cool completely.

3 Make the filling: Combine the sugar and water in a medium saucepan over medium-high heat; cover and bring to a boil. Cook, covered, until the sugar is dissolved, 4 to 5 minutes. Uncover and cook until the caramel is a dark amber color, 3 to 5 more minutes.

4 Remove the caramel from the heat and add the heavy cream; whisk until the caramel stops bubbling. Stir in the vanilla and fine sea salt. Let cool to room temperature.

5 Combine the chocolate and butter in a heatproof bowl set over a saucepan of barely simmering water (do not let the bowl touch the water). Let melt completely, about 10 minutes, then stir to combine. Remove the bowl from the pan and let cool.

6 Preheat the oven to 325°. Whisk the egg yolks and whole egg in a large bowl until frothy, about 2 minutes. Slowly whisk in the caramel, then the melted chocolate mixture. Set the tart pan on a large rimmed baking sheet; pour the filling into the crust.

7 Transfer the baking sheet to the oven. Bake until the tart is set around the edges but the center is still jiggly, 25 to 30 minutes. Transfer to a rack and let cool to room temperature, then refrigerate until fully set, at least 3 hours. Sprinkle with flaky sea salt before serving.

Index

Index

PHOTOGRAPHY CREDITS

Cover: Joel Goldberg
Food Styling: Barrett Washburne
Prop Styling: Paige Hicks

Levi Brown
Pages 14, 54, 152

Ryan Dausch
Pages 3, 32, 34, 36, 38, 42, 50, 70,
92, 94, 96, 98, 102, 104, 106, 118, 120,
148, 166

Stephanie Foley
Page 48

Mike Garten
Pages 88, 90, 142, 168

Joel Goldberg
Page 132

Yunhee Kim
Pages 16, 56, 58, 68, 80, 100, 170

Ryan Liebe
Pages 4, 60, 62, 114, 128, 144

David Malosh
Pages 78, 134, 158, 162

Johnny Miller
Pages 84, 164

Kana Okada
Page 146

Con Poulos
Pages 64, 82, 86, 110, 112, 116, 126,
136, 138, 150, 154

Kate Sears
Pages 18, 20, 40

Ralph Smith
Pages 22, 24, 26, 28, 30, 44, 52, 66,
72, 74, 122, 124

Kat Teutsch
Pages 156, 160

Anna Williams
Page 130